WHAT PEOPLE ARE SAYING ABOUT

Diving for Pearls

Who doesn't love a love story? Maggie Kay offers us a glimpse into the winding path of one who seriously explores her own spiritual life, and then reaches for someone with whom to share that life as it blossoms. Her book, *Diving for Pearls*, encourages all of us to find our way of taking the plunge.
Oriah Mountain Dreamer, Best-selling author of *The Invitation* (HarperONE, San Francisco)

Diving for Pearls is like a beautiful cloth woven from the richly colored threads of inspiring stories, insightful explanations of timeless wisdom made relevant for the contemporary world and immensely practical tips for direct personal experience. It's like Maggie Kay is right there beside you sharing her pearls so that you may find your own. Wherever you are on the journey to find love, wrap yourself up in this wise and wonderful book; you'll emerge transformed and ready for love to find you!
Julia McCutchen, Intuitive mentor, teacher and author of *Conscious Writing: Discover Your True Voice Through Mindfulness and More* (Hay House)

Maggie's *Pearls* are just that – little nuggets of wisdom that sparkle like inspirational incendiaries as you contemplate and apply them to your own life. In a marketplace that is saturated with self-help books, this is a refreshingly genuine spiritual inquiry layered with many practical insights. In addition, I think this lovely book offers one of the clearest interpretations of Buddhist wisdom that I have ever come across. I highly recommend it.
Richard Rudd, Spiritual teacher, poe
Gene Keys (Watkins)

Diving for Pearls is a lovely weave of Maggie Kay's personal journey to love and enlightenment together with practical advice on meditation, manifestation and how to open your heart. Reading it in itself has raised my vibration – a delightful way to align with this most beautiful soul.

Rachel Elnaugh, Entrepreneur, author, former BBC TV's *Dragons' Den* 'Dragon' and co-creator of SourceTV

This book is a delight! It is a wonderful mix of love story and 'how to find love' guidance. With insights into spiritual wisdom and an easy, accessible approach to meditation, *Pearls* is packed with inspiration and tools to help you manifest your ideal match. If finding love feels like a shot in the dark, *Diving for Pearls* is a must read.

Dawn Breslin, Best-selling Hay House author, speaker, coach and founder of Harmonizing

Diving for Pearls

The Wise Woman's Guide to Finding Love

Diving
for Pearls

The Wise Woman's Guide to Finding Love

Maggie Kay

BOOKS

Winchester, UK
Washington, USA

First published by O-Books, 2017
O-Books is an imprint of John Hunt Publishing Ltd., Laurel House, Station Approach,
Alresford, Hants, SO24 9JH, UK
office1@jhpbooks.net
www.johnhuntpublishing.com

For distributor details and how to order please visit the 'Ordering' section on our website.

Text copyright: Maggie Kay 2016

ISBN: 978 1 78099 865 7
978 1 78099 883 1 (ebook)
Library of Congress Control Number: 2016954757

A CIP catalogue record for this book is available from the British Library.

Design: Stuart Davies

Printed and bound by CPI Group (UK) Ltd, Croydon, CR0 4YY, UK

We operate a distinctive and ethical publishing philosophy in all
areas of our business, from our global network of authors to
production and worldwide distribution.

CONTENTS

Diving for Pearls is dedicated to my beloved soul mate, husband and best friend, Patrick Edgecombe.

Holy Cornishman

Your eyes declare you
Oh creek-boy
Fisher-man
(As you would have us know)

Who won young battles and charmed the girls
Kicked against those who would pin you down
Shrugging them off to find your own way
Dreaming on the water, listening to the tides

Yes, your eyes betray you, wild one
At once the guise of Cornish roguery is undone
Revealing the sweet, sweet heart that is the truth of you
More delicate than the gentle river breeze

And in your eyes I see an ocean universe
A place of immensity traversed by you
The wisdom of those travels, shining
The passion of those heartlands, burning

Yet so tender, your gaze upon my face
And I, too, am undone
Naked, innocent, beautiful
Before such eyes

Written by Maggie for Patrick on his birthday 4th April 2003

Acknowledgements

Thank you to all of you dear family, friends and colleagues who have supported me on this writing journey. Your love, belief and encouragement mean the world to me.

My mum, Moira Gibson, and my sister, Katy Clarke, deserve a special mention for their constant enthusiasm and intelligent interest in my vocation, along with tenacious positivity and faith in me.

So does my beloved husband, Patrick Edgecombe, for holding the certainty of my writing destiny so uncompromisingly throughout long years and many ups and downs.

And my friend Iessaiah, whose prophetic vision of me publishing "volumes of books" came at a time when I really needed confirmation of my soul purpose and has spurred me on ever since.

Huge appreciation goes to Julia McCutchen, my brilliant conscious writing mentor. I thank my lucky stars that I was guided to attend Julia's conscious writing retreat and then won her mentoring scholarship prize in 2014. As we both recognized, it seemed *Pearls* 'was meant to be written' and we were simply cooperating with that imperative. Having been tinkering with writing my first book for many years, I truly wonder if I could have finally done it without Julia's exceptional support and expertise.

Many thanks also to Wanda Whiteley, founder of Manuscript Doctor, for her excellent critical review of the first draft of *Pearls*. Wanda identified that I was essentially writing about love and helped me shape, clarify and improve the finished work enormously. Thanks, too, to Judy Piatkus, founder of Piatkus Books, for recommending Wanda to me and for friendly support and guidance along the way.

My friend Amy Webb delivered way more than the 'call of duty' when I asked her to read the second draft of *Pearls* and let me know what she thought. As well as loving it ("I couldn't put it down!") she gave very useful feedback and suggestions including an unexpected copyedit. So a big thank you goes to Amy for her enthusiastic input which was particularly valuable as I prepared the final draft.

Thank you to my dear friend, artist and Thrivecraft coach, Charlotte Turner, for painting a stunning, powerful and inspired commission for the front cover of *Pearls*. The image is mesmerizing, capturing the profound energy and message of *Pearls* in a way only a talented artist friend who deeply understands my work ever could.

A bow of profound gratitude goes to my Buddhist teachers and mentors, especially: Sangharakshita, founder of Triratna Buddhist Order; the late Himalayan Tibetan lama, Dhardo Rimpoche; my ordination preceptor, Sanghadevi; and Ratnavandana, my most treasured spiritual friend. Each has given me riches more precious than words can express and which continue to pour through me decades later to benefit many others. I thank them from the bottom of my heart.

My deepest love goes to my son, Jamie Cleland, whose appearance in my life has been totally transformational and one of the most powerful spiritual gifts of all. I so enjoyed this lively, cool and spirited boy as he grew up and am enormously proud at the amazing man he has become. I thank him forever for choosing me as his mum. Thank you, also, Jamie's dad,

Colin, for being such an exceptional and constant friend and wonderful father.

Finally, thanks to my beloved late dad, gran and first love John, who continue to love, guide and inspire me from 'the other side'.

Preface

This book is part true love story and part how-to guide. In these pages, I take you with me on the spiritual adventure of my life and share how I eventually found what I was longing for – deep trust in my own inner wisdom and a true love, soul mate and life partner that can meet me on all levels. Along with the story, I share the insights and learning that lit the way for me with the hope that this will also help illuminate your path of love and wisdom.

My quest for wisdom began when I was a child, trying to figure out if church had the answers to life's big questions. Continuing by studying psychology at university, I was profoundly affected by the death of my father and discovered the practice of meditation. For nearly two decades thereafter, I trained for and became an ordained Buddhist.

But wisdom wasn't enough. Although denying it for many years, deep down I also ached to be properly partnered by a soul mate – a true love that shared every aspect of my life. A series of experiences finally brought me to fulfill that destiny and the ensuing spiritual renaissance resulted in the resigning of my ordination and the founding of Thrivecraft – an inspirational coaching practice providing a universal path of love and wisdom for all.

Echoing my own journey, the first half of *Pearls* is about inner wisdom. Along with this part of my story, I share tips and teachings on meditation, mindfulness and intuition so that you too can tune in to your own natural inner wisdom.

The second half focuses on finding true love and includes my

'Get Ready For Love' step-by-step guide. I also describe how inner wisdom continues to serve a deepening relationship once you've met a partner (or, indeed, reveals when it is time to move on).

It is my dear wish that you will be inspired by my story and tips, transported by a special 'Ask Your Inner Wisdom' meditation I have created and recapture your natural entitlement to be completely guided and supported in all that you do. Go ahead and find the kind of love and wisdom that you so desire and so deserve. Dive for your pearls – they are right here and they are all yours.

Maggie Kay

THE INVITATION

It doesn't interest me what you do for a living.

I want to know what you ache for, and if you dare to dream of meeting your heart's longing.

It doesn't interest me how old you are. I want to know if you will risk looking like a fool for love, for your dream, for the adventure of being alive.

It doesn't interest me what planets are squaring your moon. I want to know if you have touched the center of your own sorrow, if you have been opened by life's betrayals or have become shriveled and closed from fear of further pain. I want to know if you can sit with pain, mine or your own, without moving to hide it or fade it or fix it.

I want to know if you can be with joy, mine or your own, if you can dance with wildness and let the ecstasy fill you to the tips of your fingers and toes without cautioning us to be careful, to be realistic, to remember the limitations of being human.

It doesn't interest me if the story you are telling me is true. I want to know if you can disappoint another to be true to yourself, if you can bear the accusation of betrayal and not betray your own soul, if you can be faithless and therefore trustworthy.

I want to know if you can see beauty, even when it's not pretty, every day, and if you can source your own life from its presence.

I want to know if you can live with failure, yours and mine, and still stand on the edge of the lake and shout to the silver of the full moon, "Yes!"

It doesn't interest me to know where you live or how much money you have. I want to know if you can get up, after the night of grief and despair, weary and bruised to the bone, and do what needs to be done to feed the children.

It doesn't interest me who you know or how you came to be here. I want to know if you will stand in the center of the fire with me and not shrink back.

It doesn't interest me where or what or with whom you have studied. I want to know what sustains you, from the inside, when all else falls away.

I want to know if you can be alone with yourself and if you truly like the company you keep in the empty moments.

By Oriah "Mountain Dreamer" House from her book, *THE INVITATION* © 1999. Published by HarperONE, San Francisco. All rights reserved. Presented with permission of the author oriah.org.

Chapter 1

Dipping a Toe

First Taste of Meditation

"Did that happen to you too?" I eventually gasped when I opened my eyes after the meditation. I was somewhat startled and embarrassed at what my maiden experience had just delivered. But the other participants in the meditation class simply smiled vaguely at my outburst. Only the twinkle in our teacher's eyes told me that perhaps my experience wasn't so strange.

Not that I was able to put it into words anyway. I had just been doing what I was told to do – sit still, close my eyes and focus on my breath. At first it was just nice and quiet and relaxing, but then something else started to happen. With every breath in, I was increasingly filled with a gorgeous sensation that almost had me swooning. Soon my whole body was exploding into smithereens of ecstasy – not what I was expecting from meditation at all!

I looked up at the great golden Buddha statue emanating peace around the room. Surely that wasn't what his serene smile was all about? I would soon find out, but as yet, I had hardly even registered that I was at a *Buddhist* center. I wasn't interested in religion at this time in my life. As a 19-year-old psychology student, I considered myself to be a social scientist. Meditation was only of interest because I wanted to learn more about the power of the human mind.

Here in the first floor shrine room of the Glasgow Buddhist Centre the burning incense was doing a decent job of covering up the spicy smells from the Indian restaurant downstairs. I quite liked the faint pulse of Eastern music that made it up through the thick carpet we were sitting on. The rumble of city traffic was also just discernible through the triple glazed windows, yet it seemed we were cocooned in stillness. What an exotic, peaceful sanctuary I had happened upon in the middle of my beloved Scottish home city.

It was January 1984. I was a third year student at university where I was taking a degree in psychology. The last few months had passed in a craze of partying having split up from my first love and left my home town. I relished my own piece of cheap rented freedom in the city, but suddenly, in the middle of a New Year party, I realized I didn't feel very happy. Looking around at the dingy apartment and lack of attractive men to distract me, it dawned on me that, actually, not far under the surface, I felt empty.

And so, clearing my head during a week's skiing trip, I made a complete about turn. When I returned, I stopped partying, became vegetarian and was a regular at the gym. The veggie recipe book I found in my student flat mentioned meditation which sparked my curiosity, however, it was my new yoga class that gave me my first taste.

Actually, not quite my first...

Mind Stretch

I was 11 when I decided to try out all of my local church 'Sunday Schools' for children to see what was on offer. I did not find much to inspire me, but the experiment did its job; I concluded that I was not convinced by what was being taught and adopted my dad's mantle of scientific skepticism. There was always an easy tolerance between the female churchgoing members of my family and the male agnostics, but for now, I had picked my side with the men.

That year, my older brother, Jim, found some instructions for meditation. We tried it out, earnestly holding one ear, then the other and then both for 10 minutes each, breathing quietly. It could have been a yoga practice, or more likely, one of my brother's typical practical jokes, but the effect was rather good. Whatever it was, an abiding memory of the stillness of that half hour is with me to this day.

Despite my dad's current intellectual position on religion, I was later to form the opinion that he was suppressing a rather mystical nature – reinforced by discovering that, as a youngster, he had spoken of becoming a Minister of Religion.

Mum went to church every Sunday and prayed at night before sleeping. Like most of the female members of the family, her spiritual principles were down-to-earth, warm and easygoing. Our parents had agreed that my brother, sister and I would have the freedom and opportunity to make up our own minds about what we believed in and practiced.

Dad used to expand our minds with trips to the observatory to see the stars in the night sky, and with fascinating accounts of the evolution of the human species. My imagination was stretched and exhilarated in contemplating such infinite space and time. Having enormous faith in human endeavor, Dad was excited about the scientific and technological breakthroughs of his era and furnished us with a magazine called *World of Wonder* which we children loved to read every week.

What blew my mind most of all, however, was Dad's story about his near death experience when he was very sick as a little boy. This is something he had completely forgotten about until he read the *Reader's Digest* break-through feature on the subject 35 years later. After reading the magazine article with shocked recognition, he couldn't wait to share his long buried childhood experience with us.

When Dad was eight years old and very ill with asthma, he had an experience of "floating out of his body" into the corner of the ceiling from where he could see his mother and doctor bending over him in his sick bed. From this vantage point in the ceiling, he was then drawn through a tunnel of light where he felt intense love and peace before returning to his body again. The most striking part of the whole thing, he told us, was an indescribable sense of "understanding everything".

The fact that my uber-scientific dad could testify to having had this experience gave the phenomenon 100% credibility in my eyes. But even without that, as I listened to his account and read the article for myself, I had a sense of resonance; a deep knowing that such limitless wisdom consciousness was part of me, part of all of us. It was inexplicable and impossible to prove, but I knew it was true.

Chapter 2

Wisdom Consciousness

Expanding Your Inner World

We have all had those moments. Suddenly, you are totally absorbed in a thing of great beauty – an incredible golden sunset on a beach, a piece of heart-soaring music that moves you to tears. The rest of the world disappears. There is only this wonderful experience, filling you, thrilling you. Anything you were doing pauses. Anything you were thinking melts away. You are transported into vivid aliveness and feel like you are standing in the center of the universe, that you *are* the universe.

This aliveness is your natural state. It is waiting beneath and below all the complicated layers of your life ready to greet you. All you have to do is remember to drop in from time to time – visit the oasis, refresh yourself and take that aliveness back into your everyday life. Somehow, then, your troubles aren't quite so troubling. You feel like your emotional batteries are charged up. You can see more clearly how to deal with things.

One way of deliberately dropping in to your inner experience like this is the practice of meditation. It is so easy to forget your natural, alive state that it helps to do something routinely to remind yourself. So, you build reminder time into your daily pattern – get up, brush your teeth, have a cup of tea, and meditate – and that way you don't forget to remember!

As little as 10 minutes spent like this every day can invite the aliveness back into your life.

Relaxing your body, calming your mind and opening your heart is wonderful enough, however, it is just the beginning of your inner journey. Pretty soon you will discover that your inner world gets bigger and bigger and bigger until a whole vast universe reveals itself within you – and it is just as big as the one outside.

Pulling Yourself Together

Buddhism describes four levels of experience we can access when we allow ourselves to drop into our inner world. Integration is the first level. This is where you gather all your disparate thoughts, feelings, energies and attention into one unified whole. The Buddha, the enlightened master who originated Buddhism more than 2,500 years ago, said that this first level was like mixing soap-powder and water into a ball-shaped mass. All the powder is dissolved in the water and all the water is soaked up in the powder.

Basic meditation brings about this state of integration and we cannot progress any further without it. The mindfulness of breathing practice is often one of the first meditations we come across because it specifically helps with this. We pay attention to the breath and draw our whole attention around it, strengthening and exercising our 'integration muscles'. When we feel sufficiently together, whole and clear, it lays the ground for insight and inspiration to arise.

A Refreshing Source of Creative Ideas

Inspiration is the second level. This is when you experience a bubbling up of energy and inspiration from deep within you. The Buddha described this as like a calm lake being fed by an underground spring.

Once we have unified our energy into a congruent whole we feel peaceful. But it is not a dull, static peace; it is alive. Sangharakshita, my foremost Buddhist teacher as founder of the Triratna Buddhist Order, named one of his books *Peace is a Fire*. This captures the nature of true peace very well – a dynamic, passionate, beautiful inner flaming. This is the stuff of artists, creative ideas and scientific breakthroughs. Our inspiration rises up from mysterious inner depths and takes great leaps of imagination.

Inspiration is also the path of ease.

A great spiritual principle is the law of least effort. If we are flowing with inspiration, the best way forward is effortless, expansive and joyful. We tend to miss this in our 'hard work' praising cultures. It is a commonly held belief that goodness and reward only come from difficult and punishing work – possibly a hangover from the Protestant Reformation where hard work was taken as a sign of being one of the 'elect' to be accepted into heaven. But, truly, work is meant to be a buoyant pleasure, a natural outpouring of our talent, creativity and desire to give to others.

A remarkable spiritual teacher, my friend Richard Rudd, writes about the "effortless genius" inherent in each of us in his revelatory book, *Gene Keys*: a unique, profound and rigorous synthesis of spiritual wisdom from all cultures and eras, structured around the teachings of the *I Ching*.

Richard's teaching on Gene Keys elegantly demonstrates that, truly, we need only relax into our natural talent and stop trying to force ourselves into being something that we are not. There is no need for 'hard work' and pushing against the river, nor the need to exploit others to work hard for us.

We are all made differently and enjoy what we are uniquely designed to do, cooperating with others so that everything gets done. This is the path of least effort, yet it is also highly creative and efficient. This is inspiration in action and results in a life full of synchronicity, joy and ease.

Feeling Good Through and Through

Permeation is the third level of higher consciousness that can be accessed in meditation. When you are completely immersed and surrounded by an experience of integration and inspiration, you become peaceful, energized and flooded with happiness. The Buddha's metaphor for this was of lotuses growing in the peaceful lake with the underground spring, completely immersed in and surrounded by water.

This is a mystical state where we feel we are part of something much bigger than ourselves. We have access to a higher consciousness which can be experienced as something outside of our self or as something deep within. Either way, we have access to another dimension of wisdom and guidance. In this mode, we are able to find mysterious answers to all our questions and problems. This is the gateway to inner wisdom.

Emitting Positive Energy

Radiation is the fourth level. This is when you have an unbreakable aura of equanimity emanating from you and are insulated from negative influences. Your meditative momentum is so powerful that nothing can touch you or break your mood. The Buddha said it was like taking a dip in that peaceful lake on a hot day and then wrapping yourself in a cool, clean robe afterwards.

By now, you are a transmitter. Your very energy affects people and transforms the world for the better. This is why yogis, wanderers, monks and nuns living in seclusion have a powerful part to play in changing the world even although they are removed from society. They do it by telepathy.

The phenomenon of radiation is also why crowds flock to the feet of a great spiritual teacher just to sit in their presence. This 'darshan', as this radiant presence is called, is enough to touch your soul and change you forever.

Chapter 3

Grit in the Oyster

A Visit from Dad

On June 4, 1982, 44 years after his boyhood near-death experience, Dad made an out of body journey along the tunnel of light once again. But this time he didn't come back. Having been in poor health for a lot of his life, he finally passed away aged 52. A few nights after his death, I suddenly sat bolt upright in bed. At first I thought I must be dreaming, but my eyes were wide open and I was awake. I could see an eerie star-like essence flowing from under the bedroom door, along the floor and forming a person-sized pillar at the end of my bed. I knew it was Dad. I could *feel* him.

As I stared at the essence, I was enveloped in a reassuring cloak of love and security, and for the first time since he'd died, the awful, brittle fear I had been experiencing melted away. It seemed that Dad's spirit had purposely come to me to soothe me. At once I became peaceful and fell asleep.

The evening before Dad died, it so happened that my sister Katy, my brother Jim and I were all visiting him together. Mum was delayed and would see him later on her own. We found Dad agitated, restless and a bit delirious. We hadn't seen him like that before and were puzzled, but we didn't guess what it meant. Nonetheless, we all said goodbye with special tenderness. It was to be our last goodbye.

The next morning, Mum woke me in my attic bedroom with a call from downstairs. "I've just heard from the hospital," she said, her voice cracking with emotion. "Your dad's condition is deteriorating."

We were in the middle of a rare Scottish heat wave. Ra-Ra

skirts were in fashion – short, frilly little wraps of cloth that hardly covered your backside. Mine was silky blue with thin white stripes, a welcome change from my tomboy jeans. Having dressed quickly in response to Mum's urgent call, it was my Ra-Ra skirt I found myself wearing as we sped along the motorway to the hospital in the bright sunshine.

Halfway through the 20-minute journey, I suddenly doubled up with an inexplicable pain across my body. It only lasted for moments, but felt like a signal. When we arrived at the hospital we were ushered into a waiting room. "I am sorry to tell you," the nurse said to Mum gently, "that your husband has just passed away." Shock hit me like a great crashing wave.

Where is He?

We were shown to Dad's bedside. The curtains were parted and I struggled to comprehend what I saw. He wasn't there! My dad was just not there! Sure, there was an inert shell that resembled what he had been, but this was not my dad. I had never seen a dead body before and, in that instant, I understood that it is pure spirit alone that brings life to our puppet bodies.

I stood back and looked up. I could feel Dad all around us in the air. It was as though I was breathing him, floating in him, drinking him. It was a draft of heady, intoxicating bliss. Dad was free. He was everywhere.

Back in the waiting room, the atmosphere of spiritual intensity was expanding until it filled every space. It was as though molecules of sublime gas were being pumped into the room until the density almost burst down the walls. Dad's love was all around us and he was flooding us with his presence. I looked out of the window, awestruck and suppressing an enchanted smile.

What I was experiencing now seemed more real than the talk and interaction that was going on around me. It was like my camera lens on life had been refocused to a different dimension.

My 'normal' reality had receded to the background while a vivid supernatural reality was sharply present instead.

I had never known anything like it before. Or had I? It was a glimpse into another kind of consciousness, yet there was something strangely familiar about it. It was wonderful. It was home.

Chapter 4

What Is Inner Wisdom?

Beyond Intelligence

There is a level of consciousness which lies on a different frequency, level or plane from intellectual understanding. The intellect is important, however, there is another faculty which can answer questions and find solutions more gracefully and profoundly. The stratum, deeper than the intellect, is where inner wisdom is found.

We all have a capacity for inner wisdom, but not everyone has found *access* to it. If I have a mission in life it is to help as many people as possible do so, because the positive ripple effect is enormous. With inner wisdom in charge we solve problems – we sort out communities, we sort out businesses, we sort out society, we sort out health, we sort out everything! Should we simply be able to commune with that inner guidance system, we can make all our decisions wisely and with love and for the best.

The reason many of us do not have access to our inner wisdom is because we have not encountered the means and the mechanics. We have not been in the right culture, not met the right people or the right teachers. We have just not been exposed to the opportunity to open up to that. If we are not used to contacting our depths and our wisdom then we just use what we have, which is our wits and our intelligence. This works up to a point. We human beings are highly skilled at working out how to manage life, deal with challenges and problems and get through, and we do.

However, if we are not very aware or conscious and are operating at a superficial level of ourselves, then we are making decisions that may not be in our best interests. We are making choices and decisions automatically in 'headless chicken' style and are being driven by unconscious beliefs, thoughts and fears. These beliefs, thoughts and fears are not in our awareness, so we do not know that we are being driven by them.

We then justify those actions, thoughts and beliefs with our intellect. We come up with all sorts of 'rational' and 'logical' reasons why we are doing something and may get very adamant about it, but actually, what is driving the logical justification is an unconscious emotional impetus. This means we are not really free. If we are being driven by something other than our conscious self, we are not really masters of our destiny.

Head or Heart?

The ancient Buddhist Indian language of Sanskrit has a lovely word, citta (pronounced chitt-ahh) meaning both heart and mind. The philosophy is that heart and mind operate as one and both need to be touched and transformed by spiritual practice. If anything, our heart is more dominant than our mind because it is our emotions that prompt the direction of our thinking. We habit-ually form opinions that justify what we are feeling and protect our insecurities from being challenged.

We think that we are being logical and impartial, but if we stand back and observe, we will see that there is nearly always an emotional charge driving the logic that runs through our mind. The stronger the emotional undercurrent, the more rigid and attached we are to the opinions that support our argument. Very intellectual people are particularly skilled in dressing up less conscious emotions and presenting them as compelling logical, empirical arguments.

The Buddha taught that when you are sufficiently self-aware, you no longer have any emotional attachment to your intellectual opinions. You still have opinions and can possess a searing intellect and have good debates, but you do not take challenges personally or need to cling on to your views in order to save face.

Not long after I was ordained as a Buddhist, a controversial book was published by one of our senior Order Members. I strongly disagreed with the book's arguments and thought the topic important enough to merit a direct challenge. So, I wrote a long letter to the founder and head of the Order, Sangharakshita, and requested a meeting with him.

I was quite emotionally charged when we met, but we talked about my letter and I expanded my views in more detail. Sangharakshita received what I had to say with genuine interest and calm intelligence. After we had talked for a while, he accepted my point of view and agreed that we had very different life experiences to draw our conclusions from. Furthermore, he indicated that he was always open to being persuaded to other conclusions should he be presented with convincing enough arguments.

Then I realized that I was seeing something I had rarely seen before. As well as being highly intelligent and forthright in his opinions, this man was absolutely not attached to his views whatsoever. It is quite hard to describe being in the presence of this kind of non-attachment. There was just no personality, no ego, sticking onto the conversation at all. He had no personal investment in anything being this way or that, no axe to grind, no point to prove. None! So, the upshot was whatever the rights and wrongs of his views, I left that meeting thoroughly impressed. This was why he was my teacher.

Where Does It Come From?

When practice of meditation deepens we can experience a mystical state where we feel we are part of something much bigger than ourselves. We have access to a higher consciousness that can be experienced as coming from outside of our self, or as something deep within. Either way, we have access to another dimension of wisdom and guidance. In this mode, we are able to find mysterious answers to our questions and problems.

So, is this wisdom and guidance literally coming from an outside source, or coming from our own inner source? Sangharakshita taught that it could be seen either way as this wisdom transcended inner and outer distinctions. It was probably more useful to think of it as coming from outside of ourselves, however, it depends on our personal orientation.

Some people are 'faith types' and are more heart and devotion orientated. Faith types may respond more to the idea that spiritual wisdom comes from outside and allow themselves to be receptive to those 'external' forces. On the other hand, 'wisdom types' are more head and thought orientated. Wisdom types may be more resonant with the idea that they are mastering their own inner powers rather than opening up to external forces.

I have come to understand and experience the act of downloading spiritual wisdom as a co-creation between both inner and outer dimensions. Spiritual intelligence does come from both inside us and outside us at the same time. If we stay rigidly within our everyday limited awareness, we cannot access deeper wisdom. However, if we fail to recognize our own spiritual depths and only honor external powers, we do not claim our full potency.

To ignite the spark of spiritual download, we need to do something both active and receptive. We first 'put the request out there' by posing the question to the universe and in doing so open ourselves to a greater, limitless consciousness. Secondly, being prepared to receive an answer means we are being receptive and this allows us to drop deeper inside ourselves. In this way, we participate in a cooperation between both inner and outer dimensions. In truth, inner and outer universes are all one.

100% Intention + 100% Surrender

This reminds me of a universal principle that I often share. It is the same teaching that Esther and Jerry Hicks (Abraham-Hicks) elucidate in their wonderful book, *Ask and It Is Given*. It is a magic formula for successful manifestation which allows us to create whatever we desire in life, including inner wisdom: 100% intention + 100% surrender = manifestation. In other words, when we add our 100% intention to an attitude of 100% surrender, we create the ideal conditions to manifest whatever we desire.

There appears to be a paradox when we put intention and surrender together. How can we be 100% intentional – clear, active, out there, bold, masculine, yang – and at the same time be 100% surrendered – receptive, allowing, patient, trusting, yielding, feminine, yin? But both are necessary. We need to be clear but we also need to be allowing. Mastering this juxtaposition truly is a powerful spiritual art which yields great riches in life.

Without one or the other, we get an imbalance. If you look at many spiritual practices, you will see that they contain both elements – the clarity and the boldness, but also the letting things be as they are, to allow ourselves to be surprised and receive things in ways we did not expect. A lot of us are very good at the 100% intention, but the 100% surrender side of the equation needs more attention. It is the more 'feminine' aspect of surrender that most of us need to develop more.

One of the main meditations I teach is a manifestation practice, first popularized by Dr. Wayne W. Dyer in the 1990s, which involves both intention and surrender. In my observation, many of us remember to ask, but then forget to receive. We conduct ourselves so briskly that what we request just bounces off of us, because we are not in a receptive mode. So yes, both intention and surrender are equally important in this magical formula for a flourishing life.

Letting Go into the Unknown

When she attended one of my workshops in recent years, former 'Dragon' from BBC TV's *Dragons' Den*, Rachel Elnaugh, was talking about her experience of being coached by me and said, "I don't know what happens, but so much was unlocked and other stuff just fell away. It's interesting to do that energy work because you can't describe it, you can't explain what happens. And that bothers me."

I was glad Rachel mentioned this because it gave me the chance to talk about something quite interesting about utilizing inner wisdom. Many of the people I work with, particularly self-employed entrepreneurs and single parents, are strong characters. They are organized and capable and used to being in leadership and control mode, both in their personal and business lives. However, the invitation to engage with our inner wisdom requires a degree of surrender into the unknown, into the unfamiliar, and to allow ourselves to be supported by other forces and other things bigger than us.

When Rachel and I first met and filmed a video chat about our common interest in metaphysics (the laws of unseen energy of which inner wisdom is a part), she observed that people can be unsure of such practices because it feels like doing 'nothing'. I added that engaging with metaphysics can feel like *losing control*, and that is why people are wary of it. To really gain from our inner wisdom, we need to learn to be comfortable in the unknown, allowing ourselves to be held in the unknown.

When we allow ourselves to be held in and supported by something much bigger than ourselves, it means that we can relax a lot more. We can play and have a great time and magic things along the way. This more surrendered approach to life which allows inner wisdom into the picture is, I believe, part of a new emerging way of how we are increasingly going to be working and running businesses and conducting our lives in the future.

Ethics, Meditation and Wisdom

One of the key teachings of Buddhism is the Threefold Way which describes the relationship between ethics, meditation and wisdom. This teaching is very helpful in understanding what inner wisdom is and how we can find it. The basic premise is that wisdom arises from meditation which in turn has been built upon ethics.

So, if we want to be wise, we first turn our attention to our everyday behavior and practice being ethical in our actions, speech and thoughts. In Buddhism, being ethical is about cooperating with the natural moral code of the universe, i.e. love rather than harm. The more we are aligned with the inherent loving order of our self and all things, the more ease, happiness and freedom we experience. There is no God to appease and no concept of guilt and punishment, just the natural consequences of being more or less aligned with a loving universal order according to the laws of karma (action and consequence).

An ethical person is therefore a happy, balanced, relaxed person. There is less inner and outer conflict in their life which makes it easier to drop into meditation. This is why it is sometimes better to go and do something like have a refreshing walk in nature, bringing nourishment and self-love into our body and soul, rather than force ourselves to meditate when we are feeling very disturbed and anxious. Meditation itself can soothe us, of course, but if our ethical stance is too out of balance, this requires us to go back and address that first before we can get back to meditation.

Once we have sufficient momentum with our meditation, insight and wisdom arise. Insight into the true nature of things has the effect of making us more ethical anyway, as it brings in its wake reservoirs of patience, understanding and compassion. How can we blame or harm another (or ourselves) if we experience that we are 'all one' and that everyone is doing their best, regardless of how estranged from love they have become?

In this way, a positive spiral is created between ethics, meditation and wisdom. We become more ethical, meditate more deeply and easily, and have increasing insight and wisdom, which automatically makes us behave more ethically, and so on. Eventually, we become completely enlightened – irreversibly awakened to our full potential as a human being – naturally kind and ethical, calm and meditative and profoundly wise.

Chapter 5

Wading In

Taking it Deeper

When Dad died, I was in the middle of my first year of exams at university. Trying to set out the arguments for and against the existence of God in my philosophy exam paper paled into insignificance compared to what I was going through. Fortunately, the summer holidays were nearly upon me, and I had a few months to recover some passion for my studies.

Despite an initial impetus to study journalism, I dived in to social science with relish. I soaked in all the theories, all the studies, all the claims, and all the arguments, and tried to work out what I thought. No matter how deeply I penetrated my subject, however, it seemed that for every argument one way, there was an equally compelling argument the other.

By the time I learned to meditate at the Glasgow Buddhist Centre, I was more than halfway through my degree. But even though I loved what I was learning, I was getting frustrated with all the clever word games and the academic obsession for establishing scientific proof for everything. It seemed that for every theory, there was another proving the exact opposite, and the most interesting things you just could not prove either way. There were some ideas that I found intellectually thrilling, but even with those I felt like I had gone as far as my thinking mind could take me.

Free Will and Determinism

However, there was one mystery that I just could not stop wondering about – are we humans in charge of ourselves and our destiny, or are we just robots mindlessly acting out whatever we are brainwashed with? The philosophers call it the 'free will versus determinism debate' and theories about it are at the core of much of our belief systems. Fortunately, I was about to make a new discovery that was going to give me a whole new way of understanding what we are all about and what we are capable of – meditation.

One day, my fellow student friend suggested that we go and learn how to meditate. It was something I had been thinking about having had a taste of meditation at my yoga class. So I agreed to attend an introductory course with her at the local Buddhist center. We learned two basic meditations – the mindfulness of breathing and the development of loving kindness – and I took to them like a duck to water.

I was just knocked out by meditation. So THIS is how you can go beyond intellectual thinking! A whole new dimension of experience was opening up before me. I loved it. I loved how good meditation made me feel and how clear and calm my mind was and how open my heart became. That year's exams seemed so easy in my new focused, positive state of mind. And as for Buddhism, the more I found out about it, the more fascinated I became. It was even better than psychology.

The principles Buddhists follow derive from an enlightened teacher, an actual, historical man called Siddhartha Gautama, who lived and taught in India more than 2,500 years ago. He is known as the Buddha, which means the Awakened One, as he 'woke up' and 'saw things as they really are' after a long spiritual inquiry involving deep meditation.

The idea is that all of us can become enlightened, i.e. awaken to our full potential as human beings. There are no commandments from God to obey, just guidelines from a wise, wholesome, kindly teacher to help us create happier, more fulfilled lives, or to put it more in terms of traditional Buddhism, to escape from suffering.

Best of all, Buddhism provided me with an answer to my question about whether we have free will or whether we just act out blindly from our conditioning. The typical Zen-like answer was... both are true! Hah!

Sangharakshita described this phenomenon in terms of "mind reactive" and "mind creative". The premise is quite simple. The less aware we are, the more subject we are to conditioning influences (mind reactive). On the other hand, the more self-awareness we possess, the more free will we possess (mind creative).

In other words, if our minds and hearts are very dull and asleep, we don't know what we are doing or why, and go about our lives in automatic pilot. If, however, we wake up our hearts and minds with something like meditation, we breathe awareness and therefore *choice* into our lives. We have enough inner space and wherewithal to recognize our options and make a considered decision. Meditation creates awareness, which creates choice, which creates free will.

Mind Reactive and Mind Creative

It was no wonder that I was obsessed with this free will and determinism debate at university. Every subject I was studying asked the same questions: Are we free? Do we choose our destiny? Or are we just products of our conditioning, brought up a certain way, with certain genetics and it is all going to just happen and that's it, we might as well just give up on attempting to direct our lives?

So it was a total revelation when I heard what Sangharakshita had to say about mind reactive and mind creative. The reactive mind is the one that is automatic and acting from something that we are not fully conscious of, therefore not necessarily making the right choices. The creative mind is a mind that has information, it has pause, it has self-reflection and self-awareness and therefore a choice can be made from that space, from that pause.

Many people act reactively, but with meditation, with pause, we open up the opportunity to be creative. It is almost like time slows down. You may have had this experience if you have meditated. You open your eyes and all the colors are brighter and everything seems more alive and there is more space around everything. If somebody irritates you, you don't get that charge immediately inside you because you have some sort of inner resource which allows you to see it from another perspective and you can respond from that wiser perspective.

So, with meditation we are developing that space, that creative mind, that awareness, so that our choices become more conscious and, therefore, in our best interests. The thing that determines the difference is awareness. If we are aware, if we have consciousness, then we have the freedom to choose our response to things. If we are unaware, if we are caught up in habits, then we don't have the freedom and we are victims of our conditioning.

It is interesting that the word reactive and the word creative are made up of the same letters, just rearranged!

Meditation helps us create this 'gap'. I don't know what I would be like if I hadn't been meditating for more than 30 years – a very different person, I expect. Meditation stills the mind so that you are not on automatic pilot, you do have a gap to respond from. It is a practice. Just like getting fit at the gym, if we are out of condition, we need to go to the gym for a bit before we are really adept at it. It is the same thing with meditation. When we sit down and meditate, we are literally exercising our awareness muscles, our capacity to be aware.

Chapter 6

Meditation Is Easy

Gently Does It

One of the biggest mistakes people make with meditation is *trying* too hard. The language often used to teach meditation doesn't help – "concentrate on your breath", "watch your mind" – it reminds us of forcing ourselves not to daydream in order to pay attention to a boring lesson at school.

Mistakenly, we think we are being asked to bear down on our brain like a vice and force distractions out of the way. We attempt to obliterate stray thoughts and feel like we are failing when a constant stream of insistent nonsense cavalcades through our mind. But this is not meditation; it is merely a recipe for a headache.

I prefer a much gentler, inclusive approach. Rather than feeling like I have to squeeze thoughts or daydreams out of my mind, I spend some time just relaxing and being interested in what is going on. Instead of clamping down and excluding unruly thoughts, I expand my awareness until it is so huge I comfortably include every thought, feeling and sensation I am having. Then I discover that everything is just fine the way it is or isn't, and I don't have to *do* anything. Phew, what a relief!

This is why the meditations I guide usually begin with a period of relaxing and noticing. Once we have become comfortable and relaxed and have a basic sense of the rhythm of our breath, we gradually include every aspect of our experience into our awareness and into the vast space of our breath. Then we can take our whole being on the meditation journey without any wayward rebel parts of ourselves digging their heels in.

To include our whole being like this, we start by noticing

everything we can hear and smell and taste and touch and how this makes us feel. Then we notice what our mind is up to, and gently invite our mind to have a pause from all that thinking for a while. (Our mind probably hadn't even registered that having a pause was an option before.) Finally, we tune in to our emotional mood via our heart and include that too – even if it is not a happy mood, even if we don't want to meditate. And all of that thinking, feeling, sensing and knowing is now included in the breath, included in the growing space of our overall awareness, included in our whole deep being.

Get Everyone on the Bus

Spending time like this is so worthwhile. Every aspect of our experience has a place, and needs to be included. Otherwise it will simply oppose our deepening meditation and overall direction. It is a bit like rounding up a rabble of children for a bus trip. If there is one child whom we haven't noticed needs to go to the toilet, or another who hasn't had a chance to say goodbye to his mum yet, there will be trouble. Give the kids what they need first, even if it is just a bit of acknowledgement that they would rather not be on the bus trip at all. That way there will be relative peace and the bus can at least set off for its destination without someone running away and holding everyone up.

The quality of attention that is great for meditation is gentle and allowing and receptive. It is less like concentrating for an exam, and more like getting lost in a beautiful piece of music. Instead of 'watching' the breath like some sort of army major, you might prefer to 'listen' to the breath to encourage that sense of receptivity. My personal favorite is to 'swim' in the breath (probably born of my experience of scuba diving where you are literally doing that). That way I can surrender and float in the vast ocean of the breath, becoming totally immersed in the rhythm of the waves.

Keep Clear and Focused

However, it is important not to let go so much that you forget what you are doing and why. Even as you let go into the vastness of your experience, remember to feel, to stay in touch with, a sense of direction and purpose as you meditate. Balanced meditation is like carrying a little bird safely in your hands. You don't want to squeeze too tight and hurt the little bird, but at the same time, you don't want to let your hands go too loose in case the bird flies away.

Similarly, balanced meditation requires both focus and breadth. It needs focus in the sense of being clear of what you are doing and why and remembering the purpose of the meditation. And it needs breadth in the sense of being inclusive of your whole experience, relaxing rather than squeezing and forcing. And so, before you start meditating, always clarify what you are doing, how long you are doing it for, and find some sort of anchor (like your breath) to come back to when you drift off.

The image for the right balance between focus and breadth came to me when I was in the middle of an intensive meditation retreat many years ago. I imagined that I was a mermaid (okay a scuba diver, but mermaid was more poetic and that's how it came to me at the time!) swimming deep underwater, holding a lantern in front of me. The light led the way, cutting through the darkness purposefully. In the light's wake, many sea creatures and plants were illuminated. I was aware of all the wonderful colors and forms around me, but I didn't get so drawn into them that I stopped swimming or dropped the lantern. Instead, many of them started to follow along on my great underwater sea journey.

Another clue to our focus and breadth balance is our hands. If we are sitting with one hand resting on top of the other, palms up, with our thumb tips touching (Buddha style), we can use this as a barometer of our balance. Check on the tension between our thumbs. If they are forcing together so that the thumbs start to point upwards, we need to relax. If they are drifting apart from each other, we need to sharpen up a bit.

Calming a Busy Mind

Some people say, "I'm just no good at meditating." "I can't sit still and my mind is all over the place." Well, I have a couple of tips. The first thing to say is that energetic, active people are just as capable of meditating as peaceful, docile ones. My foremost Buddhist teacher, Sangharakshita, used to say that it is easier to calm down an overexcited, energetic person than it is to stimulate someone whose energy is very locked up or repressed. Take heart!

In fact, most of us experience times when we are stirred up and overexcited and find it difficult to settle down. It is just a matter of preparing for sitting meditation in a different way.

I find that having a dance or a run or just jumping up and down a bit can really help to discharge a bit of raw energy. Running or swimming can be very meditative anyway and I would even go as far as saying that some people are better off meditating while they are engaged with something like this rather than sitting down. Personally, I love 5Rhythms dance. This is a free-expression moving meditation practice that gets me into similar states of peace and clarity as sitting meditation.

Another fantastic vehicle for our raw energy is our voice. Singing is great, but chanting can be even more effective. If we know a chant we can repeat over and over again it gives expression to some of our pent-up energy, and somehow this brings our energy into harmony and we calm down and can meditate more easily. It is said that the voice unifies the heart and mind.

You might like to try chanting the popular Buddhist mantra, "om mani padme hum", the mantra (sacred sound) of the Buddha of compassion, Avalokiteshvara. Om mani padme hum literally translates as "om, the jewel in the lotus, hum" and has a poetic meaning of finding the treasure of yourself as you open up the lotus of your being. You can use a simple repeated tune or just chant in monotone.

It probably doesn't matter what you chant. There's a lovely story about a Buddhist disciple mishearing the mantra yet getting enlightened chanting, "om mani padme cow" instead of "om mani padme hum". Another simple option is to repeatedly chant one of the ancient Indian 'seed' sound syllables like Ah, Om or Hum.

If you find that your mind is still a bit overactive once you are in sitting meditation, there is something else that can be done. As you follow your breath, pay particular attention to the sensation of your breathing low down in your abdomen. This brings your energy down out of your head and helps you settle. On the other hand, if you find that your energy is low or you are feeling sleepy, bring the attention up to where the breath first enters and leaves your body – your nose and mouth. This wakes you up and stimulates you.

Waking Up from a Dead Zone

Strangely enough, the tips for low energy, sleepy would-be meditators are pretty much the same as for overactive ones; we need to move our body. Moving the body puts us in touch with our feelings more authentically. If we move about a bit we may discover that we are low because we are unhappy about something and have shut down our energy or gone numb to avoid feeling it. Yet it is really a relief to get in touch with our feelings and have a good cry or rant. Of course, it may be that we simply need to sleep because we are tired, in which case, have a nap. However, it is okay to meditate while feeling sleepy and it can sometimes help us drop our habitual thinking. Whatever our feeling is, include that background into our meditation. Get pain or tiredness or unhappiness onto the bus too.

Accept Your Feelings

When we meditate, the main thing is that we relax. We relax physically, emotionally and mentally and that allows a deep, restorative, natural energy to flow through our body, heart and mind. I often encourage myself to let go into this state of rest and open-ness by remembering the simple Zen saying, "Body like a mountain, heart like the ocean, mind like the sky."

Of course, quite often when we pause and begin relaxing for meditation, we realize how painfully tense, hard-hearted and busy minded we are. Initially, it can be uncomfortable feeling and acknowledging this. No wonder we would rather just stay frantic and numbed out. But if we know that it is important and helpful to melt anyway and ride the waves of discomfort for a short while, we soon find ourselves feeling better. Bringing some honest, loving attention to our self is the fastest way of feeling at peace with our self, no matter how we started out.

When I sit down to meditate and realize that my shoulders are painfully tense, or I am feeling bad about something, or mentally rerunning a difficult conversation I've had, I surround that pain with a big cloud of loving acceptance. I realize that the pain will not kill me – it is just a pain, a bit of discomfort. Soon, I am not lost in the pain, but gentle and curious about it. That, in itself, is soothing and the pain quickly loses its intensity.

Be Settled and Vast

Even once we have relaxed a bit, we may still feel like our head is all over the place, thinking about a million crazy things. The truth is we probably conduct much of our life like this. It is just that we have not paused long enough to notice. My goodness, what does that mean about the decisions we make? Who is in charge?

The great gift of meditation is that it provides us with enough calm and inner space to make sure that we are choosing what is right for us. Once we practice giving ourselves this mental wherewithal when we meditate, our mind gets the idea and is much calmer and clearer as we go about our daily life. It only takes a few days of meditation to experience this and the results are wonderful.

One of the images I have for our crazy mind is that it is like one of those model snow scenes inside a glass globe. Most of the time, life is shaking the globe and all the bits of glitter snow are whirling around furiously inside. When we meditate it is a chance to put the globe down for a while, and allow all the bits of glitter to gently float through the liquid and settle on the ground. Then we can clearly see the details of the scene through the liquid.

There is a Buddhist analogy which describes this mind clearing phenomenon in another way. An elephant dropping into a small pool of water makes an almighty splash, but an elephant dropping into a vast lake only makes a relatively small splash. When we meditate, we create huge lakes of calm consciousness, so that when the 'elephants' of our everyday preoccupations drop in, we have a vast body of water within us acting as a buffer. Every time you meditate you are topping up your lake and you are giving yourself more equanimity as a resource.

Changing Your Whole World

When I was first learning to meditate, I was always amazed when I opened my eyes after a few minutes of meditation and looked around the room again. Everything seemed more beautiful – the colors more vivid, the shapes sharper and the forms more pleasing. How did the transformation come about? It is the same room as before, after all. Of course it was me who had transformed by letting the inner whirlwind subside and being able to see things more clearly and accurately. This is what meditation can do for you. It can change your whole world in an instant.

It is said that one minute of meditation cancels out hours of 'bad karma'. Meditation is so powerful and so pure that even a small amount of it undoes a lot of bad habits and purifies us very quickly. So even if we only do a short meditation, the purity of that act is so powerful that it is transformational, changing our state of mind and, therefore, the course of our life for the better.

This reminds me of a tale about a selfish king who wanted to carpet the whole world to save his precious feet from getting sore. "Why not just carpet his feet instead?" an astute aide suggested. Then, wherever he walked, the whole world would feel carpeted. We can carpet our feet like this; wrap our consciousness in meditative wisdom so that we can experience the whole world differently. By taking responsibility for ourselves like this and without harming anyone else, meditation is a most profound yet peaceful way to radically change the world.

Chapter 7

Deep Diving

Deeper and Deeper

As it turned out, I meditated formally at least once every single day for two years, then pretty much daily for the next couple of decades. That is not to say that it was always smooth sailing.

Sometimes I didn't really feel like it, or when I sat down to meditate, I felt uncomfortable and restless. Fortunately, I had been taught well and knew that this was par for the course. I would continue anyway, staying open and curious to whatever resistance or unwillingness was around for me that day. I soon learned that underneath any uncomfortable experience a deeper feeling was hiding. As soon as I allowed myself to experience that deeper feeling (usually something I would rather not feel like anger or insecurity or anxiety), I settled and felt much better for letting it out of the bag.

I was at a point in my life when I could throw myself in to this process of inner discovery. It went very well with my studies and I didn't have a partner or children or a demanding career or money or health worries or a house to maintain – I was free. Even at that tender age, I recognized how fortunate I was to have stumbled across Buddhism and meditation.

Having found a deep and satisfying spiritual path and to have a sense of such meaning and purpose just as my adult life was getting off the ground, I felt truly blessed. I loved the Triratna Buddhist community I was part of and its vision of creating 'the new society' – a refreshing interpretation of how to live, work and practice as a contemporary Buddhist in the Western world. I wanted to experience everything 'the movement' (as we called it) had to offer.

Eleventh Hour Anxiety

During my last year at university, I had an attack of 'eleventh hour anxiety' before my final exams. I was in good company. Even the Buddha was beset with severe self-doubt on the very brink of enlightenment when an apparition of himself appeared before his eyes and challenged his right to gain enlightenment. In response, the Buddha touched the ground (you often see Buddha figures in the 'earth touching mudra' or gesture) and the Earth Goddess rose up to bear testament to his years of practice and preparation for this moment. All at once, his apparitional antagonist twin disappeared, and Siddhartha Gautama broke through, finally becoming the Buddha, the Awakened One.

These days, I tell this story of the Buddha's enlightenment often as it so beautifully illustrates what often happens when we are on the edge of a breakthrough. Often our very worst doubts and fears play out just as we are about to make a significant change for the better. I am forever reminding my friends, family, clients and myself that if we find ourselves in this sort of last minute panic, it could be that we are on exactly the right path and doing extremely well. If so, take it as an encouraging sign and keep going.

Another way of describing this phenomenon is to say that our fearful ego – a basic survival attack/defend mechanism serving our lower evolutionary needs – gets stirred up when it knows that our big, free, wise self is about to take us beyond what is familiar. Our ego throws a tantrum, taunting us with our worst fears, in the way only our very own ego could, undermining our attempts to break free of its limited parameters.

Fortunately, this time I didn't succumb to my ego's frightened pleas. I caught up with my course work, completed my exams and graduated in the summer of 1985. Thanks to my tutor's encouraging advice, I have a good honors degree to show for my four years of academic dedication.

That September, now aged 21, I set off for a new life in London. The decision to move had come suddenly that summer in the middle of an inspiring puja (sacred ceremony), at the Glasgow Buddhist Centre. Much as I loved the city of Glasgow and living in Scotland, I realized that I wanted to put myself at the heart of the most happening place in Triratna – where there were women Order Members and the best conditions to train for ordination. This meant moving to Triratna's flagship community in the UK's capital city of London.

Chapter 8

Priming Meditation

Decide What You are Doing

Before you start meditating, be clear how long you will sit for and what kind of meditation practice you will do. Have a silent watch or clock within sight so you can open your eyes and check the time if you need to. You may notice that you soon don't need a clock. Before long you will instinctively 'feel' that the time you've allocated is up and it's time to come out of meditation.

Choose Your Time

It makes a big difference if you can stick to the same time to meditate every day (or every other day or every week – whatever routine you establish). If you pick your time and stick to it you don't have to keep remaking the decision to meditate and figuring out when. It just becomes part of your day or week.

First thing in the morning is great. It is well worth getting up half an hour earlier to give you this start to the day. Some people prefer last thing at night when everything is over. Or perhaps your best time is when you get home from taking the kids to school, or maybe before dinner. Whatever time that you pick, have a comfortable tummy, neither too hungry nor overfull. Choose your time and make it part of your daily or weekly routine.

Find Your Quiet Spot

Find a place where you can be quiet and undisturbed. Be in a room on your own (unless others are meditating with you).

Unplug your phone and switch off your mobile. Be out of earshot of TV or radio. Let others know to leave you in peace.

It is nice to set the scene for yourself. Perhaps face a garden window or a vase of flowers or an inspiring picture. You can burn some incense or essential oils. Make this your special meditation spot. You will find that this place will start to have a peaceful atmosphere, a meditation 'vibe'.

Be Comfortable

Find a chair where you can sit comfortably in an alert, upright position. A dining room chair is good, or an easy chair. You can also prop yourself up at the head of a bed. Undo any tight clothing, buttons or zips.

Wherever you are sitting, support your back with cushions so that your spine is reasonably straight and your head and neck are free. If you are on a dining room chair you can put a cushion under your feet. If you are in an easy chair, check if you prefer having your legs folded up cross-legged. If so, make sure your knees are supported with cushions if needed.

Some people like to sit on a pile of cushions on the floor or on a meditation stool. If so, put a blanket down first as a mat, then your cushions or stool on top. Two or three firm cushions are about right. At the right height your back is not bowing or arching but relatively straight. You can straddle the cushions like a horse, or sit with your legs folded in front of you cross-legged. Support your knees by tucking extra cushions under them if they don't reach the ground so you can relax at the hips.

However you sit, you should have a strong base – a tripod of your backside and your two knees. Have your hands resting in your lap. Tying a shawl or scarf at your tummy gives a little shelf to rest your hands on which is ideal.

There is always the option to lie down on a bed or the floor if you think you would be most comfortable like this. The only drawback is that you may find yourself feeling sleepier than if you were sitting upright. Nonetheless, the number one priority is that you are comfortable. So if lying down is what is best for you, that is fine.

If you get stiff or pins and needles while you are meditating, gently and slowly move and re-position yourself and carry on. However, the idea is to find out how to sit completely comfortably for an extended period of time without having to move, so keep playing with your posture until you get it just right.

When you are settled, close your eyes lightly, or have them slightly open if you are very sleepy or disoriented.

Let Your Weight Drop Down

Take several big, long, deep, deliberate, audible breaths. As you breathe out, let your weight drop down through the sitting bones – down, down, down through your seat and the floor into the ground.

Even as we let our weight drop down, we are also aware of an invisible force supporting us upright. It is as though we have a taut string attached to the crown of our head, reminding us of our natural poise and alertness. The more we relax and drop down, the more we feel effortlessly supple and upright.

Relax and Soften

Relaxing further, roll your shoulders a few times each way. Then move your head gently from side to side. Make some wild faces to release your face muscles. Let your jaw hang slightly slack and your tongue be free. You can use your hands to gently massage your jaw, cheeks and forehead.

Carry on over the scalp and down the back of your neck. Give your shoulders a bit of a squeeze then stroke down your arms to your fingers. Continue with a brief sweeping touch over the whole body from head to toe. When complete, you can hang over your toes for a while. Keep breathing easily and slowly uncurl.

Finally, shake out your hands and finish with a nice stretch. Come back to a relaxed, upright sitting posture again.

Take a few more strong breaths. Let your tummy be soft. Check your jaw is still slack and that the tongue is free.

Drop into Your Breath

Notice how you are breathing now, however it wants to come and go. Feel how it is to be breathing, how you feel inside yourself and the rhythm of the breath as it comes and goes. Let yourself be filled with breath. It's as though your whole body is breathing, expanding and contracting with every in and out breath. Feel your breath right down to your toes, to the tips of your fingers, to the roots of your hair.

Give Your Head a Rest

As you're breathing, you may be aware of questions and preoccupations rippling around in your mind. It probably feels like it is going on in your head. However, invite your thinking mind to rest for a little while. It is not needed for few minutes.

Soften your eyes, let your eyes go soft and dewy (even though your eyes are closed you can do that) and let the brain itself feel slack in your head. Just feel the breath going in and out of the body. Breathe in and out and let all those thought particles fall through the breath like dust particles falling through the air in a sunny room. Let them fall to the ground.

Feel into Your Heart

Breathing into the body, notice how you are physically feeling around your heart area in your chest. Can you feel if it is tight or relaxed? Can you feel if your heart area feels pleasant, or if it feels painful, or somewhere in between? Can you feel if your heart feels far away or if it feels very vivid and acute and present?

And whatever it is or isn't, just noticing it as you breathe. Feel the texture and the tone of your heart. You might be aware that there is a kind of atmosphere, an emotional atmosphere around your heart. You might not have a name for it, but you can feel its ambience, its flavor.

Perhaps you can even sense its color – the color of your emotional heart right now. You might not see it exactly, but whatever occurs to you is the color of your emotional heart right now. Even if it is not what you expect or not what you want, notice the color or colors.

Being with All That You Are

Continue to breathe with all that you are – all that you think, all that you feel, all that you sense, and all that you know. Gather yourself into the breath and let yourself drop into the vastness of your total being. Getting into this zone is a meditation in itself, and you need do nothing more. However, you are now also ready to take it further into a focused meditation if that is what you've chosen.

Chapter 9

Pearly Queen

Community Life

The London Buddhist Centre, or the LBC as we called it, was Triratna's leading edge center in the world at the time. I had never remotely considered moving to 'the big smoke' of London before, but I wanted to be where the biggest and best facilities were, wherever that was. My youthful enthusiasm was rewarded by the offer of a room in Samayatara, the newly created 'ordination hothouse' women's community and a job in one of the right-livelihood businesses, Windhorse Typesetters. I was thrilled beyond imaginings to become part of such a fascinating spiritual, economic and social adventure.

Following the vision of Triratna's founder, Sangharakshita, my fellow spiritual friends and I practiced a radical, semi-monastic, total lifestyle, creating the 'new society' – a world within a world. One of the main features of this lifestyle was 'the single-sex principle'.

The idea behind this is that it is more spiritually advantageous for us to live, work, study and practice with members of our own sex. It was purported to be less sexually distracting and to remove conditioned ways of relating to the opposite sex. We could still have opposite-sex sexual relationships if we wanted, or same-sex sexual relationships for that matter (the Order was semi-monastic rather than monastic, after all), but the emphasis was on deepening spiritual friendship with our own gender.

Although I found this very strange at first – having always been a tomboy, enjoyed more typically masculine activities and been closer to male friends until then – I could see the point and was willing to give it a go. In fact, it was very liberating and honest. In the process I made very close women friends, gaining a much deeper respect and understanding of my own sex, and therefore, of myself. Peculiar though it may have been for twentieth century Britain, I am very grateful for having experienced this social-spiritual living experiment.

A Londoner by birth, Sangharakshita had spent 20 years in India where he studied and practiced Buddhism from teachers of all Buddhist traditions, becoming a monk and a wandering holy man in the process. An amazing scholar and author, and now a gifted teacher himself, he returned to the UK in the 1960s and set up the Friends of the Western Buddhist Order (FWBO) – an exciting, modern and relevant application of the core principles of Buddhism. In recent years, the FWBO has been renamed Triratna.

Here at the LBC in the 1980s and 1990s, a couple hundred of us lived in a dozen or so big shared Victorian houses scattered around Victoria Park in east London and/or worked in what we called 'right-livelihood' businesses. These were ethical, cooperative businesses run using Buddhist principles, including a vegetarian café, a bookshop, a typesetting business, a whole food shop, a secondhand/recycling shop, an ethical gift shop, a complementary health center, an arts center and a housing co-op. The Buddhist Centre itself was a renovated Victorian fire station, reclaimed from squalor in the 1970s by the first generation Triratna disciples. It was an urban village spiritual utopia that I rarely stepped out of.

I absolutely loved it. I felt happy and fulfilled, inspired by the teachings, lifestyle and friendships I was experiencing, and expanded by the constant insights and personal development that resulted. Every moment of the day was meaningful and enjoyable – our collective morning meditations, companionable work, intense lunchtime 'tête-à-têtes', fascinating evening classes and friendly bedtime chats back home.

One thing Triratna really gets right is its emphasis and

practice of spiritual friendship and skillful communication. We were living, working and meditating together, peeling off layers of superficial persona, revealing our true, authentic selves. There was nowhere to hide, and we got to know ourselves and each other deeply and intimately. That, in itself, was massively satisfying and transformative.

A Trip to the Himalayas

After a three-year stint working at Windhorse Typesetters, I became restless and decided I needed to explore the world a bit more. And so, I got temp jobs working for the big banks in London's financial sector a short cycle away and saved up for a 10-week trip to the Himalayas. In February 1989, age 25, I was on a plane bound to Kathmandu in Nepal.

Following my first few days at the Triratna Kathmandu teaching outpost, I set off trekking with a good friend who was passing through on her world travels. We had an amazing time and all too soon I was saying goodbye to her. I was on my own now. I spent a few days relaxing at a lakeside guesthouse before heading back to Kathmandu for a couple of weeks' retreat in a Tibetan Buddhist community. I was preparing myself for what was yet to come – a pilgrimage to Kalimpong in Sikkhim to visit Dhardo Rimpoche, one of Sangharakshita's most venerated Tibetan lama teachers.

Pilgrimage

My legs were aching trying to hold the semi-crouched position Rimpoche had asked me to adopt for the empowerment ceremony. As he was speaking in Tibetan, my instructions came in broken English from my kind and friendly host, Jampal, acting as interpreter. Regardless, my concentration was intense and the atmosphere in the room charged like the dense moment before a lightning strike. Something incredible was happening.

I guessed it did not matter too much if this clumsy big Western woman wriggled and wobbled while we recited and chanted. But that was barely my concern right now. I was finally here, in the presence of the greatest living spiritual being in the world, as far as I knew at the time. It had taken me nine months of mindless work in glamorous City of London financial HQs to save enough money for the trip, not to mention the arduous and eventful journey from London (via Bangladesh, Nepal and India) to reach this remote hermitage in the Himalayan mountains of Kalimpong.

The colorful, cluttered little room was pungent with sweet Tibetan incense. Wisps of it were visible, floating in the bright morning sunshine coming in through the windows. A tiny half-Chinese half-Tibetan elderly man, Dhardo Rimpoche, sat cross-legged on his platform seat wrapped in red and gold Tibetan monk's robes. So sweet, humble and childlike the day before when we first met, he was now alight with crackling, formidable power and authority. It was as though someone had plugged a floppy, smiley ragdoll into mains electricity, transforming the doll into a real, live superhero intent on a mission.

Dhardo Rimpoche is one of Sangharakshita's closest and most celebrated teachers. They met when Sangharakshita was living in Kalimpong in the 1950s. A reincarnate Tibetan lama, Rimpoche is revered as a 'living Bodhisattva' (or awakened being dedicated to the happiness of all beings) having been named as such by Sangharakshita. While we had Sangharakshita on a pedestal, the awe we felt for Dhardo Rimpoche was off the scale. It certainly was for me.

Although I regarded Sangharakshita with enormous gratitude and respect – and still do – I had little contact with him and never actually felt a deep personal connection. His books and teachings rocked my world and I was devoted to his interpretation of the Buddhist teachings and embodying them in my life within

Triratna. But I found Sangharakshita distant, maybe because I felt the single-sex principle kept him somewhat disconnected from the women's wing of the movement.

By contrast, the personal connection I felt with this old Chino-Tibetan man – someone I could hardly speak to and had only spent a few hours with – was scintillating. It was warm. It was tender. And it was powerful. Being with Rimpoche was like being with Yoda from *Star Wars*. I realized, in those moments of the empowerment ceremony, that *this* was why I had come to Asia. I had come on a pilgrimage to sit at the feet of Dhardo Rimpoche.

The first time Jampal brought me before Rimpoche, I burst into foolish, star struck tears. But the venerable one put me at ease. Soon I was giving him the presents I had with me, including some gifts from Sangharakshita that I had been asked to pass on. I made arrangements to come back the next day. As I was not yet ordained, I was not able to ask for an initiation into my sadhana (a special meditation practice given at ordination), but I requested to participate in some kind of ceremony with Rimpoche.

I did not know what to expect when I returned the next day, but Rimpoche obviously knew exactly what he was doing. Despite my leg cramps and ungainly recitations, that empowerment ceremony touched something deep within me and I have never been the same since. I returned to the UK, on fire with the teachings of enlightenment, determined to turn the wheel of the Dharma (Truth teachings) for the rest of my life.

Chapter 10

Finding Wisdom

Wisdom on Tap

Wouldn't it be amazing to have help and guidance whenever you need it? The astonishing thing is that superb wisdom is right there within you, waiting to be tapped, every single day. Whether you are out shopping wondering what to buy for dinner, on the brink of a major life decision, or handling a shocking crisis, a powerful source of personal guidance is only a few breaths away.

Everyone has inner wisdom. It is part of you. It is just a matter of locating the 'wisdom spot' within you and learning how to communicate with the intelligence there in order to decipher the guidance. We have so much more of a smoother ride in life when we know how to do this effectively. But most of us do not listen to our inner wisdom, and even if we hear it, we do not know which 'voice in our head' to trust.

It is more usual to refer to what I am calling 'inner wisdom' as intuition or instinct, both of which tend to get used inter-changeably. We are just as likely to proclaim, "My intuition is red hot today," as to say, "I'm going with my gut instinct." But actually, intuition and instinct are different things. Intuition literally means 'inner tutor', the teacher within, and is part of our 'higher' consciousness. Instinct, however, derives from our more basic animal nature – our automatic, survival, flight or fight response. I prefer to use the term inner wisdom as it is less easily confused with instinct.

The trouble is that we are not very accustomed to finding, trusting and using our inner wisdom. Unlike instinct, it does not come automatically and requires a bit of cultivation. Generally speaking, these days in our culture and education systems, the emphasis is on our quick thinking rather than our deep knowing. This means that most of us are missing out on a fantastic natural method of getting the best from life.

In days gone by we knew how to commune with this guidance system, but our modern lifestyle is such that we have by and large forgotten all about it. Our minds are filled with information and external stimulation. We scurry about getting more and more confused, taking wrong turns and running in circles. No wonder we do not feel so good, that something is missing in our lives.

Fortunately, not everyone has forgotten how to tune in to this excellent natural source of guidance. Countless spiritual practices, sages, and mystics have kept the art alive through the ages. In recent years, there is a renewed wave of interest and understanding sweeping our planet. More and more of us are picking up the threads of these ancient ways and weaving them together with fresh spiritual intelligence to make a modern tapestry, a complete map, which works meaningfully and practically for us today.

Stop and Ask Meditation

Stop for a moment, just a moment. It's okay. It's really good for you. Take a deep breath…

Breathe out… Take another deep breath… Breathe out…

Is there somewhere you can sit down for a few minutes? Or a quieter place to stand?

Decide to take a few more minutes to yourself. Breathe freely. Stretch, shake out, then settle again. Let the tension sigh away as you breathe out. Be at ease.

Where are you? Look around. See the colors and shapes around you. Then close your eyes if you can do so safely. Breathe in the air.

What can you smell, taste? What can you hear, near, far? Notice what you are touching. What is touching you? Notice the textures; the temperature; your feet on the ground; the air on your face; the way your clothes wrap your body. Breathe in and out through your senses.

Breathing into your whole body, let your weight drop down, down into the ground.

Let your breath move through you. Soften your muscles. Let your shoulders drop, your tummy be round, jaw loose, tongue free. Feel your breath reaching your toes and running along your spine. Feel your breath arriving at your fingertips, washing around your scalp.

With your breath swimming through you, let go of thinking for a while. Give yourself a delicious time-out. There is nothing to figure out for now. Let your eyes be soft and dewy. With the mask of your face melting and your brain feeling slack, allow your thoughts to gently float to the ground, like dust particles falling through a sunny room.

Feel how good it is to breathe – to just be breathing. There is nothing else you need do right now. You are just breathing, sensing, being.

Feel your chest rise and fall. What is it like in there – tight, expansive? Allow it to open a little more. Breathe into the area around your heart. Does it feel good, uncomfortable, or numb? Just breathe. However it is or isn't.

Feel any upset. That's okay. Feel your good feelings. That's okay. Feel your blankness. That's okay. Whatever you feel or don't feel. That's okay.

Breathe into the whole of yourself – every molecule, every vibration, your body, your mind, your heart. Let yourself drop deep. Let yourself spread wide. Let the breath be everywhere.

Notice the space inside you, the warmth, the places that feel good. Breathe. Allow them to expand. Feel the freedom within you. Let it grow. Know that everything is going to be okay. Feel the vastness within and around you.

Being with all that you think, all that you feel, all that you sense, all that you know.

Be with all that you are.

Now, what is bothering you? What is on your mind – a decision, a problem, a question?

What is it? What is troubling you? Choose one thing that you would like to resolve.
Breathe with all that you are. Make it clear in your mind what this one issue is.

Feel the energy of it in your body. Feel the emotion of it in your heart, in your breath.

Now imagine yourself picking up your issue and rolling it into a pebble in your hands.

There is a beautiful, deep, clear pool of water before you. After a moment, make a wish to resolve your issue and drop the pebble into the pool. Let the pebble sink down, down, down to the bottom of the pool.

Just being for a while, enjoying the ripples.

Then… you notice. There seem to be some messages coming from the ripples. What whispers do you hear? What images appear? What ideas occur to you?

It may not make sense. It may not be what you expect. It doesn't matter. Just notice.

Whatever happens or doesn't happen is perfect.

Take a few more moments to be. Breathe.

With the next few breaths, wake back up. Take a deep breath and stretch. Open your eyes, feeling whole and fresh. Wake up fully.

Remind yourself what just happened by the pool. What was your issue? What messages did you receive about it?

Whether you received any messages or not, whether you under- stood them or not, let it be as it is. You may not know how your issue will be resolved just yet. Restate your wish to have your issue resolved. Carry on with your day.

Now and over the next few days, open to whatever help or ideas come your way.

Chapter 11

Gathering Treasure

How Do I Tap into My Inner Wisdom?

Pause and take a few deep breaths.
Ask yourself what is best.
Receive your inner answer.

It is as simple as that! The profoundest guidance, answers and solutions are literally a few breaths away. The trick is to REMEMBER to pause and ask in the first place.

The best way to remember to pause and ask in the heat of your busy everyday life is to practice a little when things are quieter.

Just 10 quiet minutes a day will really help. Spend 10 minutes of every day sitting quietly by yourself – no TV, radio, phone, computer or interruptions – just you sitting down, relaxing, and feeling your breath moving through your body.

The first section of my guided meditation – Ask Your Inner Wisdom – will help with this. (See Appendix for how to download your free audio of this meditation.) Just sit back and relax. The rest will take care of itself.

If you are not accustomed to 'taking 10' like this, you will be amazed how refreshing it is and how good it makes you feel for the rest of the day.

It is good to find a regular spot in the day that works for you – like after your morning cuppa, on the train to work (providing you have earphones!), or sitting in the car when the kids are dropped off at school – and to incorporate it into your everyday routine.

Take a Few Deep Breaths

Whether you are on the go or doing something quietly, you can take a few deeper breaths and really notice them.

Breathe in deeply, all the way in, filling your lungs. Let the air out again, all the way out. And again a couple more times.

Let your breath come and go as it wants to now, following its rhythm. Notice how your tummy and chest expand when you breathe in and deflate when you breathe out. Feel the air moving through your airways. Enjoy the sensations in your body.

Fill your whole body with breath. Imagine it flowing right down to your toes, all the way to your fingertips, along your spine and around your face.

Breathe in refreshment. Breathe out tension.

Notice how good it feels to simply be alive and breathing.

Ask Yourself What is Best

Clarify your question. Keep it simple and one-pointed. (If you have more than one question, just pick one for now.)

Formulate your question into words. Ask the question in your mind, or speak it out loud if you can.

For example:

>*"Where is the best place to park?"*
>*"Would it do me good to go to this party tonight?"*
>*"Should I leave my job?"*

Gently repeat your question a few times and relax into your breathing. Then let your question go...

Receive Your Answer

The answer may come straight away or pop up a little while later. It may come in a variety of forms. Sometimes we have a sense of hearing an inner voice – we almost hear words being spoken within us – or we see an image of something or a scenario in our mind's eye. At other times we may feel a "yes" or "no" answer in the body, or have an inexplicable sense of suddenly 'knowing' a solution.

This is because we perceive the information we receive in different ways. Some of us are predominately visually orientated, some auditory, some somatic and some cognitive. In other words, some of us are more alert and tuned in to what we see, some to sound, some to sensations in the body, and some to our thinking mind.

It is the same when we are receiving inner wisdom – we may perceive and interpret the wisdom via any of these senses. (In Buddhism, the mind is considered to be our sixth sense, so inner wisdom would be our seventh sense!)

My suggestion is that you experiment with how your inner wisdom generally comes through to you. Test yourself with questions that you already know the answer to. For example, ask the question, "What color is my car?" Do you see, hear, feel or know the answer, or a combination?

Then try out your truth sensor and the typical way you receive "yes" and "no" answers. I could ask myself, "Is my name Maggie?" and "Is my name Susan?" and test out how I see/hear/feel/know my responses to both those questions. Now when you ask questions that you don't know the answers to, you will be more familiar with the way your inner wisdom communicates with you.

Many of us feel inner wisdom in our body, often in the tummy area which is why we call it 'gut-feeling'. But we can also feel sensations in our heart or the solar plexus. These areas are all 'chakras' – key energy centers in our body.

A feeling of 'rightness' is usually pleasant and expansive – a warm open-ness.

A feeling of 'wrongness' is usually unpleasant and contracting – a cringe or knotted sensation.

A direction (e.g. where to shop or park) will come as a sense of attraction towards somewhere, almost like we are being pulled by a magnet, essentially a 'rightness' warm and expansive sensation.

You will be directed away from the wrong place by a sense of repulsion – a 'wrongness' unpleasant and contracting sensation.

It is a bit like playing the game 'hot and cold' where the object is hidden and you are trying to find it while the hider directs you as to whether you are 'hot' close by or 'cold' far away.

Listen to your inner 'hot and cold' promptings and follow them.

Which Voice Do I Trust?

There is a knack to being able to identify your true intuitive voice and knowing when you can rely on its wisdom.

Reliable inner wisdom is characterized by ease, peace and simplicity.

The 'yes' or 'no' answer is deep, stable and warm. It has a feeling of certainty even if you can't explain the reasons why.

True wisdom is patient and loving, even if it is giving a "no" answer. There is a sense of compassionate understanding that everything is in its right place.

The voice of wisdom is deep, rich and resonant like a big gong. It seems to radiate from deep within the body – usually the tummy or the heart.

An unwise opinion is very different. It may come with strong energy, but there is an emotional charge to it that makes us feel tense and unstable.

Unwise opinion comes from our head and works hard to justify itself with lots of mental chatter. Our thinking may be 'spinny', confused or complicated. We may even change our minds or come up with contradictory messages.

The basic flavor of our 'un-wisdom' is fearful – either in attack or defense mode. We wear it like armor, but yet we feel vulnerable. We may be feeling adamant, but we are not truly confident.

All our emotions derive from only two things – love or fear. Love feels expansive, secure and flexible. Fear feels contracting, insecure and rigid. Wisdom comes from love while unwise opinion comes from fear. Listen to the voice of love.

Using Inner Wisdom Everyday

Here are some examples of the kind of things you can answer and find solutions to and directions for in everyday life:

At home
Deciding to move house
Finding a house
Finding lost items
Deciding on and shopping for decor/furniture

At work
Employing staff
Applying for a job
Doing deals
Creative solutions

In relationships
Finding a partner
Deciding on suitability
Making and keeping friends
Deciding on socializing

Out and about
Best routes travelling
Parking spaces
Shopping – best shops (including online)
Directions

Chapter 12

Losing a Gem

Unexpected News

The phone call came out of the blue. It was a Saturday morning, the 10th March 1990, and I was at home in my community in London enjoying the beginning of a spacious weekend. It was my first love's father on the phone and he told me he had some bad news. Bad news? More like earth shattering, life changing, stupefying news. My first love was dead. My John was dead.

In a confusion of shock, I found myself stumbling out of our Victorian terrace house, past the park gates and down the tree-lined street towards the London Buddhist Centre. My dazed, autopilot trajectory continued towards the market where the florist was. We often frequented this little shop to buy flowers for happy occasions and to decorate the shrine rooms in our businesses, community homes and the Buddhist Centre itself. I bought some white flowers, and took the shortcut back to the park gates and home.

The shrine room in our community was on the top floor overlooking the back garden, directly above my bedroom. I took the flowers up there, clearing away the old ones, and began creating a fresh shrine display around the Buddha statue in its usual place underneath the window. The special shrine room atmosphere, a profound meditative 'hum' of silence, seemed to deepen in reverence as I cleaned and arranged the sacred items.

I was joined by two or three other community members when it was done. Having heard the news and knowing John from the life story I'd shared and recent visits, they gathered to support me with a special ceremony. We meditated and I read out some words from the *Tibetan Book of the Dead*, speaking to him of how to navigate this transition through the bardo, or intermediate state, of death.

Farewell First Love

In the days and nights that followed, I dreamt of John often, my psyche reeling as I tried to come to terms with the reality that this exceptional young man, love of my teenage life, had suddenly departed this earthly plane. In my dreams John was communicating with me, explaining what he was experiencing. In one dream, his spirit flew down from the sky and took my hand, intent on taking me back up to the heavens with him. "No!" I screamed at him, shaking my hand free, and dropping to the ground again, terrified and determined to stay alive. In another, I was attending John's funeral when I saw him in the crowd, a ghostly apparition looking upon his own coffin. The impossibility of it blew my mind, and left me gasping in horrified paralysis.

Only six months before his death, John and I had connected closely again. Although we hadn't been together as a couple for five or six years, we had stayed in touch. Periodically, we sought each other out, needing to experience that special mind, body and spirit connection again. Since our teenage relationship, I hadn't found any others even remotely comparable to the intensity, passion and true meeting that John and I had enjoyed.

I was frustrated by the compromised romantic relationships I was experiencing within Triratna. Being with John was such a contrast to the noncommittal, polite, herb tea dates I was having in London. During one of my visits to Scotland, John met me at the airport in his red shiny MG, roof down under the moon. He whisked me off to his high tech pad where a champagne accompanied bubble bath was waiting. The man made me feel alive!

In recent months, however, I made a decision that it was finally completely over between us. Soon after we last hooked up, he met a wonderful new girlfriend and fell in love, proposing to her in some John-ish, hugely romantic way. I felt genuine happiness, but also relief. It was as though I could finally put him down and let another woman carry him now.

Yet, John had his deep troubles. After a bout of flu he was preparing to return to a new job he hated. No one saw him or spoke to him that night. It was before the days of mobile phones and his fiancé had been involved in a car breakdown and couldn't ring. His mum was due to phone but had got caught up taking a relative to the hospital. The next morning, she called round to his apartment and found him dead. It seems he took his own life.

So that was it. He was gone. John – sparkling, mad-eyed, hilarious, beautiful, generous, super-energetic, mega-intelligent, larger than life John – was gone. He was just 26 years old.

Chapter 13

In the Oyster Shell

A New Job

John's death hit me very hard. Re-orientating my career after that life changing pilgrimage to the Himalayas the previous year, I attended an interview to study a postgraduate degree at the London School of Economics. It was a terrible interview and I didn't get in. I was feeling emotionally trashed and physically unwell, eventually realizing that I was coming down with chicken pox. Then I got the news that my precious guru, Dhardo Rimpoche, had also just passed away. I spent the next two weeks on a thin, hard futon mattress in my bedroom in my community home feeling like I was dying myself. I have never felt so ill before or since in my life. Adult chicken pox is no joke, let alone a double bereavement.

As I was recovering, I cancelled a planned solitary retreat in a cave at a remote mountain retreat center near Granada in Spain. I just didn't have the inner resources to travel, be on my own, or abroad, let alone do a solitary retreat in a cave up a mountain. Instead, I joined my dear friend and spiritual mentor, Ratnavandana, who was living in a country cottage in Cornwall at the time.

Resting for a couple of weeks in that plump, generous, airy country house was truly nourishing. Hardly able to speak or eat, I did nothing other than feel terrible and cry. I was allowed to be and held in soulful, understanding, unconditional friendship that needed nothing in return. What an amazing gift of love, space and time. I will always be grateful for that, teaching me exactly what is needed to tend grieving loved ones in the future.

Within a month or two I was recovered and applied for a job

at Phoenix Community Housing Co-op. Phoenix was originally set up to house the first wave of Buddhists that settled in the area when the LBC was established in the 1970s. Now in 1990, Phoenix had evolved into a housing association for single people more generally, though it still housed a lot of Buddhists.

My interview was with the Chairman, Ajita, a charismatic, mystical, former street-wise Glaswegian who I had first met at the Glasgow Buddhist Centre in 1984. In fact, Ajita had been Chairman of the center when I first came along to meditation classes, and it was he I asked to lead the meditation society I went on to set up at my university. Here we were, six years later, both now living in London as part of the Triratna community.

I got the job! It was a big leap as I only had a little housing co-op experience (as my home community was part of a neighboring housing co-op), but my degree in social science, ability to write and communicate well, and experience doing PR and marketing at Windhorse Typesetters all helped – not to mention my own Scottish charm. So I became Phoenix's Housing Development Manager.

Ajita was very hands-on in Phoenix, as was his German partner, Susanne, who worked beside us in our open plan office as the Housing Manager. One of Susanne's endearing features was that she spoke English with a Scottish accent (having picked it up from Ajita), so there was a very Scottish vibe created by the three of us at Phoenix. Susanne and I also were both going through the ordination process together and we became very dear friends. Tragically, Ajita passed away in 1995, but Susanne and I remained close, especially as we were destined to follow very similar paths in the future.

In my early days of Phoenix, there were huge projects and stretches ahead, but I rose to the challenges with relish, pouring my all into my new work. In those early few months, I managed to negotiate the purchase of four large Victorian houses (housing 20 people otherwise at risk of eviction) from the council at half their market value; arranging Phoenix's first ever loan from a bank; and making winning bids for nearly a million pounds in grants to renovate many properties.

I had to hold my own with the 'big wigs' of the London social housing world – directors of housing associations, managers of financial institutions and councilors and senior staff in local government. I was a 26-year-old semi-monastic Buddhist wearing clothes from a charity shop, but carried it off with energy and confidence.

The work suited my skill set and personality. Success depended on bringing people together for a joint purpose, building belief and creating something wonderful out of nothing – a Phoenix rising from the ashes right enough. My main resources were passion and determination and a bit of a silvery tongue. Ever since then I have enjoyed unshakable belief that a bunch of people with no assets can do anything together if they put their minds and hearts together; a theme that has repeated itself through more recent parts of my life.

On the Rebound

My personal life was not quite so successful, however. It was as though a light had been extinguished in my soul. Grief made me feel mildly depressed and I was going through the motions emotionally. It probably suited me to lose myself in my work rather than feel my feelings. I was content enough living with three good Buddhist friends in our community house (having moved on from the ordination hothouse community) and being involved in activities at the LBC, studying Buddhism and going on ordination preparation retreats. In 1991 I was nearly recommended for ordination, but something was holding me back and it didn't feel right. It didn't happen.

Around then, I got back involved with a boyfriend I had been with a year or two before, Colin. We were not madly in love, which suited me. It had bothered me when we were first together that I was quite bedazzled by him yet he seemed a bit cool about me. That perceived indifference was what led to us splitting up before. But now the dynamic between us was balanced. I was more self-contained which gave him more space to be enthusiastic.

Colin was a great friend and amazing to talk to as he was such a good listener and a wise soul. He also shared the Buddhist world with me, being newly ordained himself and a full-time part of the Triratna community. It was safe to get honest with Colin about my inner world and all my feelings, which meant it was possible to get honest with myself.

I wasn't completely well, feeling increasingly exhausted and below par. By Christmas 1990, I was running out of steam. Continually stressed by the relentless pace of my work at Phoenix, I was no longer able to ward off the post-viral fatigue that was beginning to envelop me. I wasn't going to get away with being manically busy and ignoring my emotions any longer. Contemplating the possibility that I might need to cut down to part-time work, I arranged to have an extended holiday over the Christmas holidays.

Ratnavandana had now moved to another place in Cornwall, this time an apartment in a country house amidst beautiful public gardens. She was away for a few weeks, and so I went back to Cornwall again to stay in her house and do some more healing.

This time I was on my own, which was less comforting than my previous stay, but the solitude was welcome. I slept, went for walks, and dived deeply into my inner world without interruption. I meditated, drew, wrote in my journal and read *Women Who Run with the Wolves* – a groundbreaking book doing the rounds in our circles that explored archetypal female psychology.

Inspired by the book, I found myself making some drawings which were very revealing. I drew a representation of myself as a big fluffy chick that had just laid a large golden egg. Stick-like men in suits and top hats were gathering around in awe of the egg congratulating me. But they weren't really congratulating *me*. They just wanted the golden egg I was laying. The drawing made me see that part of why I was ill was that I had been pushing myself to perform and achieve to gain the approval of men in authority.

Somehow that realization broke the spell, and after that five week break, I was better again. I didn't need to cut down to part-time work. The post viral fatigue was over and maybe, just maybe, I was beginning to get over the loss of John.

Chapter 14

Wisdom for the Blues

Just a Bit of Tenderness

From time to time, I embark on a purposeful, focused spiritual program. Often it is a simple thing – daily reading, reflecting and writing on certain themes – but the effects are profound. Sometimes this is because I want to recover from challenges or make changes in my life by dropping deeper and deeper into the richness of my inner world.

The program may begin with joy and enthusiasm, but sooner or later it begins to bite. I recognize the pattern. At first there is excitement and inspiration at the juicy wisdom being studied, then times of discomfort and resistance because an unenlightened part of me feels threatened; usually hanging on to some ingrained and unconscious way of being that is really not necessary or useful anymore.

After feeling tense and unhappy for a while (which can be hours or days) it becomes clearer what is being challenged and what needs to let go. It helps to allow myself to feel my upset emotions – have a rant or a cry or whatever – and talk to someone who understands the process, or write it all down in a journal without judgment. Eventually the realizations come and I end up feeling cleansed, renewed and aligned with a more peaceful, happy way of living than ever before.

At such uncomfortable times, the best thing we can do is simply accept ourselves just as we are and without needing to analyze why we are feeling out of sorts. A great exercise when you feel like this is to write a long list of "I love me when…" and finish the sentence. Write about loving yourself, good or bad, until you have a feeling of accepting every last part of yourself unconditionally. Even if you don't feel it to be true at this time, write it down as though you do. For example, "I love me when I am inspired," "I love me when I am depressed," "I love me when I know what I am doing," and "I love me when I am confused."

Unconditional acceptance of oneself is always the beginning of the end of unhappiness. It is so simple. Even when you are feeling utterly wretched it is possible to step outside and look back upon yourself compassionately, just as you would look upon a crying child who has broken a beloved toy. The trick is to remember to do so. Once, when I was upset about something and unable to feel compassion for myself, my friend fetched a mirror and tenderly held it up in front of me. Looking at my poor, crying face in the mirror I felt rather sorry for the wretched girl I saw reflected back to me and my heart melted for her. I instantly changed and felt compassion for myself.

Eckhart Tolle's masterful book, *The Power of Now*, captures the simplicity of this awareness and acceptance process beautifully. I have read scores and scores of spiritual and personal development books over the years, but this one captures an essence of them all. I always say that *The Power of Now* is one of my 'desert island books'. If I was stuck on a desert island with only a few books, I would want this to be one of them.

There is also a wonderful loving kindness meditation that I learned many years ago at my first meditation classes, and still practice and teach with relish. It is a Buddhist meditation called the metta bhavana, or development of loving kindness. Not surprisingly, it seems to me that most spiritual traditions have similar contemplations or prayers. The meditation begins by cultivation of love for oneself, then a friend, then a stranger, then an enemy, then the whole world. In my experience it is deeply transformational as well as gently nourishing, no matter what state you are in when you begin.

I have written about love, one way or another, a lot. I suppose really understanding what love is all about is the core of my inspiration and practice. Even writing about love and compassion when I am not feeling so great has the effect of cheering me up enormously. I guess, "I love me when I am deep in challenging process," and "I love me when I am writing inspiring stuff about love." Just a little tenderness does the trick.

What Helps When You are Feeling Down?

What really helps when you are feeling down? Well, the starting point is simply this:

1. Accept How You are Feeling

The energy we put into resisting our feelings when difficult emotions are bubbling under the surface is incredible. Instead, we keep ourselves zombie-like – plodding along in a low-grade half-life – not happy, but not engaging with what is going on either.

Our habit of blaming ourselves can mean that we would rather remain in a state of brittle denial. We can't admit to ourselves that we feel this way as we would judge ourselves for being so. It is better to pretend that we are okay.

But if we can just surrender for a few moments – really allow ourselves to feel how we feel – yes we feel the pain more fully, but we also begin to let in a little love and tenderness. Much like we would if we were giving attention to a friend who was having a hard time.

Rather than being lost in this no-man/woman's-land, it is better if we can *name* what we are feeling. When we name the feeling it means that we are no longer subsumed by it. Part of us is now standing outside and looking in, and we can feel some compassion for ourselves.

And having accepted how we are, we have the option of turning towards something more positive.

2. Take ONE Tiny Step

When we are feeling down, everything can feel overwhelming. We don't WANT to do anything to help ourselves. It is all too much.

So my suggestion is this – choose ONE thing from the list below, just one. One thing that appeals a little bit...

- have a bath
- go for a walk
- make a fresh juice or a wholesome soup
- listen to a guided meditation
- get closer to nature/go outside
- confide in a good friend
- clean and tidy up
- read something inspiring
- count your blessings
- have a nap
- hang out with positive people
- enjoy some exercise
- listen to uplifting music
- pet an affectionate animal
- pray to receive support
- have a cuddle
- do something to help someone else
- channel inner guidance
- reflect on your good qualities
- make love

- look for the beauty in things

3. Take Another Step

What you will probably find is that once you've taken one step, you feel inclined to take another. And some positive momentum builds from there.

For example, one morning when I was feeling a bit under par, I decided to do one thing nice thing for myself: have a bath.

That prompted me to read some inspiring words from a book while the bath was running. After my bath I did a little light housework and made a fresh juice for breakfast.

It was a bright day and I could hear the church bells ringing, so I went for a walk, pausing at the church door to listen to the congregation singing a hymn.

On the way home I popped in at our caravan in a nearby field and told it out loud how wonderful it is and how much I loved it.

During my walk, all these 'how to lift yourself up' ideas came to me, culminating in the inspiration to write them down to share. My hope is these tips might support you too if you are feeling less than wonderful one day.

4. Find the Hidden Gem

There is always a nugget of gold buried in our difficult emotions. Our feelings are trying to tell us something, bring our attention to something that will open understanding and meaning to a situation or experience.

The hidden gem in my 'downtime' on this occasion was: a) the need to rest and restore at the end of a very busy, productive year; b) the opportunity to release some grief from the past; and c) the prompt to write down some wisdom that might be supportive to others going through a bit of 'downtime'.

5. Love is the Answer

Giving a little attention where it is due is a profoundly loving act. That is all we are doing when we honestly accept how we are feeling, truly loving ourselves just the way we are.

It gives us the momentum to take a positive step, and maybe even another and another... and opens up the possibility of gaining some wisdom and insight from our experience, some meaning, some letting go.

When I first wrote this, I cheered myself up by watching a YouTube video of a song sung by Aloe Blacc, *Love is the Answer*, which had been shared by my Facebook friend, 'healer of hearts' and author of the *Diary of an Accidental Psychic*, Mark Bajerski.

Love is the answer, that is for sure, and we need only begin with one tiny step to let it back in to our life.

Chapter 15

Taking the Plunge

Should I or Shouldn't I?

I lived and breathed Triratna Buddhism, but I always tried to keep an objective perspective. I was like a participant sociologist living in the rainforest studying an indigenous tribe; I did not want to disappear into collective customs, forgetting there was another whole world out there. What attracted me to the movement in the first place was that it was started by a ground-breaking maverick (as Sangharakshita was in his early days), and the ideas and understanding were so refreshingly free of outmoded old religious habits, customs and superstitions.

Even so, there were certain ideas promoted in the Triratna during my involvement that rankled. My main issue was with how sexual partnerships and family life seemed not to be considered ideal conditions for spiritual development. I was challenged by what appeared to be the prevalent view that succumbing to our 'biological urges' handicapped our progress. The movement was predominately male and I wondered if Sangharakshita really understood women. Worst of all, I got the impression that women were considered to be spiritually disadvantaged and more prone to 'lower evolutionary' instincts than men.

It was this apparent 'reach for the heavens and leave the lowly world behind' attitude that ultimately led me to depart Triratna. Towards the end of my years in London, I gave a controversial talk at our large open public class on the difference between the solar-masculine and the lunar-feminine approaches to spirituality. I didn't directly challenge what I considered to be Sangharakshita's solar-masculine approach, but even so, drawing attention to an alternative perspective sent shock waves around the room. (A handful of my audience, however, absolutely loved it!)

From what I have heard, Triratna has significantly changed in recent years. Certainly, lots more Order Members have paired up and are living with partners and/or are having families together. But back in my days of involvement, wariness of relationships and family life seemed prevalent. I was close to being ordained in 1991, still hugely fired up from my pilgrimage and empowerment with Dhardo Rimpoche a couple of years before. However, a talk on an ordination preparation retreat – hinting that we should undertake not to live with a sexual partner after we were ordained – slammed the breaks on. I just knew I could not promise any such thing. It took me a further two years to work that one out of my system and continue to ordination.

From when I was about 24, my maternal alarm clock started ringing intermittently, set off by the birth my nieces and nephew. Most of my female spiritual friends were not interested in having children, being quite content with Triratna's seeming encouragement to stay single and avoid family life. But for me, my instinct to have a baby became an issue, especially as I had now requested ordination. It was also at cross-purposes with my boyfriend, Colin, who was ordained and did not have family life in his sights. I discussed my baby hankerings from time to time but, by and large, tried to put it on the back burner and get on with other things.

Eventually, I resolved my dilemma when my preceptor, Sanghadevi – who would be deciding on my readiness and ordaining me – made it clear that it was fine to have a baby *and* be ordained. I just needed to do some planning, like having a career break, and do one thing at a time. This was all I needed to hear to let go of my tension and inner conflict about it. I knew for sure that I wanted to be ordained, but not if I wanted to become a mother so it seemed best to just go with what I was sure of and get myself ordained.

To be at the London Buddhist Centre was an amazing way to spend my 20s and an experience I will always be grateful for. As well as daily meditation and living and working with fellow Buddhists, I attended evening and weekend classes, had the benefit of no-holds-barred spiritual friendship and mentoring, and spent about two months a year on intensive retreats in the country. During that decade, I was thoroughly spiritually slow-cooked from the inside out.

In November 1993, at the beautiful Dhanakosa Retreat Centre on the banks of Loch Voil in the Scottish Highlands, I was ordained into the Triratna Buddhist Order and became Srimati.

Ordination

The night was electric, charged with magic. Down by the loch, the moon lit the inky water and the awesome presence of the loch-side mountain wrapped its arms around us. We were dancing, jubilant, tracing our names in the air with sparklers. They were OUR names, new names symbolizing spiritual rebirth, just announced during our public ordination ceremony. My name looked magnificent, a laser signature in the dark, starry sky:

Srimati   Srimati   Srimati

Twelve of us were ordained that year. I had been through the ordination process with many of them for years, living and working with some, on retreats and in study groups with others, and was thrilled to be sharing this retreat with two of my closest friends, Srisambhava and Dhammadassin. I was also thrilled that the ordination retreat that year happened to be in Scotland. It was a bit of a fluke as the ordination process was in transition between two retreat centers and used Dhanakosa as a one-off. How wonderful to be ordained in my native land!

During the previous week of silent retreat, individual private ordinations had taken place with our preceptors while everyone else continued meditating in the main shrine room. I was the first. I quietly rose from my place near the back of the shrine room and crept out of the barn building into the dark. My way was lit by candles on the ground along a short path to a wooden cabin, perched on the edge of the gushing mountain-river. The air was cold and crisp. I could feel every step I made, hear every breath I took.

My preceptor, Sanghadevi, was waiting inside the cabin. The shrine was dressed in silky white cloths, flowers and candles, and was aglow with sacred light. Underneath the central Buddha statue, a picture of Sangharakshita seemed like it actually contained him, as though he was there inside the frame, watching and blessing me. I took my seat on some cushions made ready alongside my preceptor and we began the ceremony.

Guided by Sanghadevi, I made my formal request for ordination and took my vows. Familiar with chanting the 'refuges and precepts' in call and response after nearly 10 years of practice, I was now about to finally become a member of the Order. And so, I promised to commit to, or 'take refuge' in, the Buddha – the ideal of enlightenment, the Dharma – the path of the Buddha's teaching and the Sangha – the spiritual community. We then chanted the 10 ethical precepts in Sanskrit, traditionally translated as:

I undertake to abstain from taking life
I undertake to abstain from taking the not-given
I undertake to abstain from sexual misconduct
I undertake to abstain from false speech
I undertake to abstain from harsh speech
I undertake to abstain from useless speech
I undertake to abstain from slanderous speech
I undertake to abstain from covetousness

I undertake to abstain from animosity
I undertake to abstain from false views

Thanks to Sangharakshita's poetic, modern, positive touch, we also recited the precepts in English as:

With deeds of loving kindness, I purify my body
With open-hearted generosity, I purify my body
With stillness, simplicity and contentment, I purify my body
With truthful communication, I purify my speech
With words kindly and gracious, I purify my speech
With utterance helpful and harmonious, I purify my speech
Abandoning covetousness for tranquility, I purify my mind
Changing hatred into compassion, I purify my mind
Transforming ignorance into wisdom, I purify my mind

Sanghadevi then initiated me into my chosen sadhana or primary meditation practice. I had chosen Green Tara, a female Buddha figure symbolizing compassion in action. Green Tara has been a constant inspiration for me ever since I first picked up a postcard depicting her in a bookshop in Scotland's capital city of Edinburgh many years before. Her image shot an untranslatable message of connection and meaning into my heart, love at first sight. I felt like I knew her, soul-to-soul, that I *was* her and she was me. I repeated Tara's mantra after Sanghadevi, "Om tare tutare ture svaha," and felt new power course through me in a direct line from Tara herself.

Finally, my new name was revealed. Personally chosen by your preceptor, your ordained name is meant to reflect spiritual qualities that you already have or are aspiring to. I knew Srimati was right immediately. It was as though Sanghadevi had dug deep into core of the earth and found the esoteric name that has always been buried there for me. I later discovered that Sanghadevi had been keeping my name secret for over two years from when it looked like I was nearly ready for ordination but then veered off course.

Radiant Mind

The meaning of Srimati drawn out for me by Sanghadevi is 'radiant mind' or 'auspicious intelligence'. Sri means radiant, glorious, shining, and auspicious. Mati means mind or intelligence, but it also means determination or devotion, so I've come to think of Mati as 'strong minded'. As my dear mum will tell you, "Oh, she is very determined alright!" My lighthearted, colloquial version of Srimati is 'Bright Spark'.

For the six days before it was announced at the public ordination, I cherished my new name privately. "Srimati, Srimati, Srimati," reverberated constantly throughout my mind and heart like a mantra. I meditated on it, wrote about it in my journal, walked along the loch-side paths with it and absorbed it into my being. This was me now! I was Srimati, 'radiant mind', a member of Triratna Buddhist Order.

At the public ordinations, I discovered that Sanghadevi had given me four 'Sri-sisters': Srisambhava, Srivati, Sripada and Srivandana. As she announced our names, Sanghadevi said a little more about why she had chosen those names for us. Srimati, she explained, had seemed an even more appropriate name for me two years after she first thought of it as I had shown such determination to continue on with the ordination process after my "wobble with the single-sex-principle," as she called it.

Sanghadevi also gave me a special link with my dear friend, naming us after two spiritual companions, Srimati and Srisambhava, from a Buddhist text on spiritual friendship called the Gandavyuha Sutra. In the sutra, Srimati and Srisambhava are two enlightened spiritual companions, a girl and a boy. Sanghadevi made the joke that it is possible to be spiritual friends with the opposite sex, it just has to be kept on a high level.

In retrospect, this whole 'living with an opposite sex partner' question has been an important and recurring motif for me throughout my life. Deep down, I have always known that I was destined to find and marry my twin soul, and that far from being a spiritual disadvantage, it would be the most spiritually potent and transformative experiences I would ever have. Back in those days, the only hint I had was my passion for a book by Stephen and Ondrea Levine called *Embracing the Beloved: Relationship as a Path of Awakening*. In naming me after a spiritual couple, Sanghadevi had inadvertently put her finger right on my destiny.

We had the public ordination ceremony on the afternoon of 25th November 1993. It was a beautiful day. Thick fluffy snowflakes fell, covering the ground in magical icing. We all dressed for the occasion, some 'up' (colorful dress and jewelry) and some 'down' (shaven head and robe) depending on the way we wanted to express our ordination. My choice was a long, straight, burgundy velvet skirt and matching cropped jacket with a mustard scarf. I later wondered if I had chosen those colors in unconscious affinity with the Tibetan monk's robes worn by Dhardo Rimpoche. My mum had excitedly helped me choose my outfit during a few days with her before she drove me to the retreat center, wonderfully supportive as always.

After the ceremony, we returned to the dining room in our finery for a lovely dinner and to open the copious amounts of little gifts we'd all given one another. Able to chat now, for the first time after days of silence, the atmosphere was sacred, joyful and delighted, and it was wonderful to call each other by our new names. With the snow continuing to fall all around us in that stunning highland location, it was like the most beautiful, fairy-tale Christmas day.

Chapter 16

Trusting Inner Wisdom

How Do We Know It Is Wisdom?

There is a question that comes up often, which is, "How do we know it is our inner *wisdom* speaking to us and not some other inner voice?" The answer relates to the awareness we develop when we foster 'mind creative'. When we are aware, we get to know ourselves. We get to see what our deeper motivations are, where we are coming from emotionally, how our conditioning has shaped our opinions and attitudes. We become lovingly aware of those things and in doing so we get more adept at choosing our responses.

Generally speaking, from a spiritual perspective, we are motivated by only two states of being. If we boil it all down, we are either motivated by love or from fear. With all the compli- cated things we feel and go through, we are either avoiding what we don't want (or trying to manage life so we don't have to encounter the thing that we don't want), or we are coming from a place of love, connection and open-ness. Wise, reliable inner wisdom is informed by love. So, my practice in trying to learn what is inner wisdom and what is not is just simply ask the question, "Am I coming from love or fear?"

Supposing, for example, you have a decision to make on whether you should accept a new consultancy contract. If you come up with an anxious response, "Oh yes, it doesn't attract me but I better accept it because I'm desperate for money," then it suggests that you are coming from fear. If your response is a happy, "I would love to work with those people," then you can recognize that you are coming from love. It sounds very simple, but sometimes all it needs is to pause and ask yourself whether you are coming from love or fear.

Another way is to do the 'tummy test'. We talk about 'gut feeling', don't we? I can be strolling around town wondering where I can buy a nice dress, and then I remember to check in with my body, the sensations in my tummy. It is like a radar, detecting whether I am getting a "yes" or "no" signal about whether I should go into a particular shop.

When we are in fear mode, we tend to feel contracted. When we are in love mode, we tend to feel expansive. So we can check in with our physical experience in our body – "Am I contracted or am I expansive?" – to tell whether or not we are in love mode or fear mode. Sometimes we can be in love mode and at the same time a bit excited and anxious. That's just some superficial fluttery stuff. Underneath, we know we have an expansive feeling.

Back in the Buddha's day, more than 2,500 years ago in India, there was a very rich culture with many different spiritual teachings, traditions and systems. Spiritual seekers used to ask the Buddha how to tell which teachings were good ones and which will lead them on the wrong path. He explained that if it is a good teaching it will lead you to freedom, to release, to openness and expansion. If it is a poor teaching, it will lead you to bondage, contraction, and shrinking.

So again, this is a very simple test – if a choice or decision leads to a feeling of expansion and freedom, the chances are you are in love mode and following inner wisdom. If it leads to a feeling of contraction, the chances are you are in fear mode and not in touch with inner wisdom.

So how does this fit with the practice of 'feel the fear and do it anyway'? If you say "no" to something because it has created fear in you, are you not then staying small, staying within your 'comfort zone' and not growing and developing?

Being aware of yourself at a deeper level helps you answer this dilemma. You might feel fearful about doing something. It might be a challenge, taking you outside your comfort zone, but having identified that, you are aware of something deeper. Often when we are changing and growing, we are confronted with a lot of scary, out of comfort-zone type experiences.

You know you are feeling fear, but you can detect that, underneath that, there is this expansive, bigger reality which is deeply motivated by love rather than fear. And so we can acknowledge the fear, include the fear, but at the same time choose to step courageously with the love. In that way, you can 'feel the fear and do it anyway'. It is subtle, but it is worth getting the hang of this more refined awareness.

Inner Wisdom and Desire

Another question I get asked about a lot is whether or not we can trust our desire and wanting. Can our ego's desire for something override our inner wisdom? In my experience, the role of desire and wanting are often misunderstood, especially in some spiritual circles. Is it okay to want? Well, yes, unless it tips into grabbing and grasping. Let me explain.

On the Buddhist 'Wheel of Life', a traditional visual representation, there are 12 segments around the circumference representing the different stages in the 'chain of conditionality'. Each one leads to the next which leads to the next and so on around and around the wheel. The important part of the chain for us is where it runs from 'contact' to 'feeling' then 'desire', 'grasping' and 'becoming'. This is the section where we have some power to make a difference and not just run on automatically around and around the wheel.

The Buddha taught that there was only one point of freedom from this endless wheel of conditioning. The point of freedom comes in the gap between 'desire' and 'grasping' – so just after you know you want something, but before you grab it. This is very subtle. You come in contact with something and you want it, and if you are not careful, you go into grasping and that takes you on around the wheel again and you are not free.

Wanting which is relaxed and not tipping into grasping is a powerful creative state. It is blissful and it takes you up a positive spiral, away from being trapped on the wheel. I have called it "havingness". Abraham-Hicks call it "eager anticipation". We are clear and bold and feel deserving in what we want, but we are also relaxed, trusting and surrendered which allows us to attract and receive what we want without grasping.

If you look at the Abraham-Hicks book *Ask and It Is Given*, it is all about embracing our wanting, embracing our desires, because that is our creativity. That is us deciding where we want to go next. That is us discovering ourselves. We are presented with things we like and things we don't like all the time, and that's how we figure out where we are going next. So of course we want – we want to be free, we want to be happy, we want to evolve. So it is about welcoming wanting, and then learning this art of havingness. Havingness is not grasping, it is not 'must have', but neither is it 'can't have'.

It seems to me that some people who follow Buddhist teachings think that you should get off the wheel *before* wanting. So they stop themselves feeling, cut off from their genuine desires and don't allow themselves to want anything, mistaking this as a practice of non-attachment. This kind of misunderstanding of Buddhism and non-attachment is life-denying and over ascetic. Even the Buddha didn't do that. The Buddha taught the Middle Way between ascetics and hedonism.

So this is a really subtle but powerful thing to understand. It is not 'can't have' or 'must not have' or 'don't deserve' or 'shouldn't have'. We are beings that want and desire and we can welcome that and "kiss the joy as it flies". That is freedom.

As William Blake wrote in his poem:

He who binds himself to a joy,

Doth the winged life destroy,
But he who kisses the joy as it flies,
Lives in eternity's sunrise.

So we are looking for eternity's sunrise. Kiss the joy! Love the joy! Love your man, love your car, love your food, love your house, love the beach. Enjoy it. Have more of it! If you want a bigger house, a bigger holiday, have it, but have it with havingness. Open to havingness. Send out your intentions and surrender to being surprised by how the Universe delivers. That is what the promise of life is all about.

If we are in a state of true havingness – open to our desires and surrendered to receiving them – we are entirely aligned with our inner wisdom and intuition. We are in love mode rather than fear mode. Our wanting becomes intuitively informed. Our wanting is wise. There is no interference with our intuition by part of us that wants something that is not wise. We are relaxed. There is no grabbing. We are in the gap between wanting and grasping and we start to rise up the spiral – and this is blissful.

We used the expression "dwelling in the gap" in Triratna. What comes from there is bliss. If you fully inhabit something, you are really in the moment – if you really see the beautiful pink color, you really feel the lovely cool breeze caressing your face – it is completely blissful. And we can't do that if we are rushing around or thinking of where we are going. If we are in the moment, it is as though time bends and everything opens up. The more we meditate, the more we enjoy the mindful gaps, the more we can enjoy life.

And the more we can see things for what they really are, the more we feel loving kindness. When we give something full attention we are loving it. And when we love something, we give it our full attention. Love and attention are one and the same thing – and inner wisdom contains them both.

Chapter 17

Unexpected Riches

Surprise!

Against the odds and ahead of hard evidence, I instinctively knew I was pregnant. As I lay in the bath there was something magical in the air. I found myself, hand on belly, making a heartfelt pledge in a tender whisper, "If you're there, you're very welcome and I'll do my best for you." It was early January 1994. I was 29 and a brand new member of the Triratna Order, having got home from my ordination retreat only four or five weeks before. Long enough to conceive a child, as it turned out!

Birth and death were very much in the air at the time. On my first Order weekend in early December, we heard that a member of the Order, Sthirika, had passed away. I didn't know him personally, but news of his death had a surprisingly big impact on me. I felt very sad and could sense him all around me, much like I could sense my dad and then John after they died. "Strange," I thought. "Maybe this is what it'll be like being bonded with my brothers and sisters in the Order now."

Then, in mid-December, one of my few close non-Buddhist friends tragically gave premature birth and lost her twin boys within a few days of each other. We had a pair of the grimmest winter funerals conceivable – dark, cold, grey and raining as their tiny white coffins were placed in the ground. There was more sadness a couple of weeks later when a fellow Order Member had a very early miscarriage, something she shared with us at the January Order weekend.

Her news prompted me to take a pregnancy test. My cycle was only a week overdue, but I had been feeling quite odd over Christmas time. After the Order weekend, Dhammadassin,

Srisambhava and I went round to our friend's flat to make the test. Five shots of schnapps (or some such untouched drink from a distant holiday) were poured at the ready and put in place around the kitchen table. I went off to do the test upstairs. "It's positive!" I shrieked as I ran back down. We drained our shots in one go.

As I worked out later, I had conceived on the very same day as the Order Member who miscarried, in both our cases, completely unintentionally. This was two weeks after Sthirika had passed away. Buddhists believe that we 'choose' our own parents, whether consciously or unconsciously, based on the karmic momentum carried over from our previous birth. I came to wonder if Sthirika was trying to find rebirth in the Order and had changed his mind about having the other Order Member as his mum and plumped for me instead.

But whether this was true or not, becoming pregnant was the beginning of a profound new experience of extraordinary love in my life. One week into my relationship with this unknown, unexpected new being, however, I was howling with an ancient grief as I bled and feared it was over. The pain of that love had begun to make itself known to me.

An Unforgettable Night

But all was well. The feelings of love and vulnerability gathered substance during the months of pregnancy. My body surrendered more and more to its task and my love for my unborn became increasingly tangible with the growth of the life in my belly. So did the fears. Dreams of the coming birth were mostly beautiful, but my heart was full of the fragility of human life. I felt I would do anything to protect this life inside me and yet there was so little I could do to ensure its well-being; that was ultimately out of my hands. Even before my baby was born, I was learning that maternal love means letting go.

On 23rd September 1994, I spent an unforgettable night bringing my son into the world. He was born at home in the women's community, Samayatara, where I'd been living again for a few years. It was Thursday, our weekly 'community night' where we all came together for the evening and my turn to cook. This Thursday, we had some guests as my Cornish friend Ratnavandana was staying to help out with the birth.

With the first chop of garlic, I got a contraction. An hour or two later, thankfully after dinner, things had progressed and we called the midwife and the baby's dad, Colin. It was turning into quite a community night with us all downstairs in the lounge, chatting and tending to me in turn, one of whom happened to be my massage therapist. I was also very glad that Colin was a trained nurse and had attended several births already.

Later, I got into a lavender scented bath. I practiced a kind of 'mindful breathing' which helped me cope with the pain. I counted my breaths, staying in the moment, realizing that each count in itself was just about bearable, but if I strung them all together, I got overwhelmed. I became so calm the midwife wondered if the labor had halted, but things were progressing well. Back in my bedroom, at 1:42am, my baby boy was born. He didn't cry, just made a little sound like a stretching cat about to settle down after an adventure.

In the calm and comfortable aftermath that night, when everyone had gone, I lay stung awake by wonder, gazing at my beautiful baby boy. The blacks of his eyes shone in the dark, peacefully apprehending his new world as he lay between us, his parents, the very flesh that had created him.

A few days earlier I'd dreamt I was begging a Nazi soldier not to shoot me, to give me one more week so I could see the face of my unborn child. Becoming a mother was showing me that the death of your child is the cruelest loss imaginable. As a practicing Buddhist at the time, such strong feelings raised questions for me. What gives rise to such powerful and self-sacrificing maternal love? To what extent does this love help or hinder us in living a spiritual life?

Chapter 18

The Wisdom of Letting Go

Hindrance or Opportunity?

Some Buddhists claim that having children is unhelpful for your spiritual development because it opens you up to such strong attachment. (Attachment is a big theme in Buddhism which teaches a path of letting go or non-attachment.) It is generally true that the more emotionally involved you are with someone, the more you are liable to be caught in attachment. At worst this can mean limiting, insecure ways of relating and unhealthy dependence. For a Buddhist, however, identifying and uprooting this 'clinging' is the very heart of practice.

But even when I was a Buddhist, I couldn't agree with the idea that having a child was spiritually diminishing. I soon came to value the power and vitality of parental love and discovered that motherhood gave me a depth of experience that enriches my spiritual life, contacting a huge reservoir of love such as I had never known before. It seemed to me that parental love is a spiritual opportunity.

The trick is not to back away from the strength of that love, but to dwell deeply in it, to penetrate love's true nature and the nature of that which you love. As a parent you have almost no choice but to love your child intensely. This demands that you find the same intensity of wisdom to match it. The more your heart is open, the more you can allow any wise reflections to touch you and let them transform you.

One story that illustrates this is that of Kisa Gotami, probably my favorite story from the Buddha's day. Kisa Gotami comes to the Buddha cradling her dead child. She is distraught, even a little crazed, and cannot accept that her child is dead. She has heard the Buddha is a great man, a great healer, and begs him to provide medicine for her 'sick' child. The Buddha replies that he will help her. She must find a mustard seed as medicine, but there is one condition – it must come from a household that has not known death.

Kisa Gotami sets out on her quest, knocking at doors. Those who greet her are happy to give her a mustard seed, but shake their heads when they hear of the condition. "The living are few, but the dead are many," they say. Kisa Gotami cannot find a house in which no one has died, and gradually a new perspective dawns. She sees the universality of death and this allows her to acknowledge what has happened. She buries her child, returns to the Buddha and commits herself to the spiritual life.

Kisa Gotami 'wakes up' during her quest. She sees that death and loss are universal, so she can finally grieve and let go of her child. This is a deeper engagement with life and death that sees it in a spiritual perspective. In accepting the death of her child, Kisa Gotami gains insight into the nature of human life. Obviously this is challenging ground and Kisa Gotami had the Buddha's help, but she did not stop loving. It was just that her love was placed in a much vaster context.

Another example comes from the Tibetan Buddhist tradition. Many of their texts dwell on the mother-child relationship to evoke the intensity of love that human beings are capable of. Mother love is used as a metaphor to describe metta, a Sanskrit word meaning unconditional loving kindness:

As a mother watches o'er her child, her only child, so long as she doth breathe,
So let one practice unto all that live an all-embracing mind.

The difficulty lies in transforming exclusive love into one that includes all beings. The prospect of loving every being like one's only child is awesome, but life offers glimpses of such an experience. For example, when we grieve the death of a loved one, the combination of feelings arising from a personal loss, with an acknowledgement of the universality of death, can open up an intense love for all humanity.

Compassion comes with realizing that all beings will one day share this moment in their own way. Similarly, dying people sometimes reach a serenity where they accept impending death and are imbued with a sublime love for their family, friends and humanity, and for life itself – as if only this fullness of love is important, more important and powerful than death itself.

Saying Yes to Love

Over the years I have thought a great deal about the nature of human love – ordinary human affection and intimacy with all its imperfections. It is this middle ground between the lofty climes of metta and the grip of unconscious attachment that I am interested in. That is where many of us stand for much of our lives.

When I first became involved in Buddhism, I latched on to the notion of non-attachment because I was hurt by loss and death. I was only 19 and didn't know myself well. Although fairly bright and positive on the surface, I was unconsciously on the run from painful experiences. My adolescence had ended abruptly with my father's illness and death. I felt mature beyond my years and my world of teenage rebellion became meaningless.

So, too, did my relationship with my first love, John, despite having held such passion and promise for me. I had thought he was the man I'd spend my life with. But soon after my dad died, my need for John melted away and I felt strangely alone. Suddenly, I found myself telling him it was over.

Although my response to Buddhism was largely sincere, I misconstrued some of what I learned in the early days. While I rejoiced in my fortune at having come across this spiritual path so young, I did not realize how much emotional backlog I had to deal with. It was during this initial phase that I developed a sort of defended pseudo-independence and fooled myself that I was free of attachments.

Fortunately meditation and spiritual friendship sorted me out when I moved to London. Meditating every day, living in community and working in right-livelihood businesses was like being in a hall of mirrors. Everywhere I looked, I saw my true self being reflected back. There was no escape. So the pain of what I had been running from caught up with me. It was a journey into the underworld and I came more deeply into relationship with the grief I had been trying to deny.

By fully grieving, in opening up my heart to what had happened, the pseudo-independence crumbled. I was heart-broken and from that broken heart a bigger heart was released. I began to see that non-attachment was not about holding back, being self-contained and trying to limit the inevitable emotional damage that comes through being in relationship with people.

Instead, I found that non-attachment is about loving deeply, letting my love flow and admitting how much friends, family and loved ones matter. It involves being willing to love them, give myself to them, even though we will one day be parted. There is nothing we can do to stop death or to end separation, but practicing non-attachment does not mean shutting off love. It means being prepared to take the pain of losing loved ones because the sheer experience of love is worth it.

My attitude to love began to change as I acknowledged the truth of impermanence and the inevitability of the suffering implicit in loving. From feeling I made myself vulnerable by loving, I began to experience a greater robustness in my love. What did I really have to lose? I started to see love as giving rather than losing myself. To really love I must be prepared to give everything and let go of everything. I must learn to release my love, love for its own sake, with no desire for a secure payoff.

A decade after my first contact with Buddhism, I had a partner and a son, and so those ponderings had a new arena. The issues of attachment were different. I couldn't choose whether or not to love my son, whether it was 'safe' to invest emotional energy in him. It was absolutely what I must and did do. I was only just beginning the journey of loving as a mother, and every time I thought I understood what that involved, it changed. Those changes brought many lessons. Only insight in to my son's true nature – a beautiful being that I love, but ultimately cannot control the fate of – freed me from attachment.

Every so often a tragic news story rips through the day-to-day illusion that our loved ones last forever, never to be disturbed by accident, illness, separation. I don't want to have to experience the same as Kisa Gotami in order to wake up and gain insight, but I do want to wake up. I want to feel unbounded love that is passionate, full and wise. Living with the tension of loving fully and letting go is not easy – simultaneously holding two apparent opposites – but it provides the ground of my awakening.

The tension does allow a larger perspective to emerge; continuing to love and let go is the only option. Love is not about binding another or oneself to a *status quo* because of insecurity. (That is essentially an impossible task as things change, like it or not.) It means taking a stand on a deeper, spiritual understanding. To love fully is to open oneself to the truth of impermanence and to totally relish our loved ones while we can, 'kissing the joy as it flies'.

Chapter 19

Diving Solo

Life Changing Miracle

My son Jamie's conception was a total, and somewhat miraculous, surprise to us. Colin and I'd had an easygoing relationship for a few years, but by the time the pregnancy test announced its astonishing news, we were edging towards going our separate ways. Despite the shock, and the complete life change that it implied, we each found ourselves inexplicably delighted about the new life insisting its way into our world.

We were both ordained Buddhists, with overlapping but independent lives as part of a modern Buddhist community in London. As such, we lived and worked in neighboring single-sex community houses and co-op businesses. Before Jamie came along, our relationship consisted of Saturday evenings catching up over an Indian meal and the night at my open-to-visiting-male-guests community. That was provided we were both in town that week. We occasionally had a holiday or a weekend together and spent Christmas with Colin's mum and dad. It was good, even if it was beginning to wane.

With the prospect of our impending arrival, however, our slow drift apart came to a halt. Colin dropped plans to move to Amsterdam and I let go of an idea to relocate to Edinburgh. It was an easy mutual decision to stay in London and find a place to live together and bring up our child. And so we became a family unit. The first couple of years were occupied by establishing a home, changing working arrangements, and adapting to the whole magical adventure of being parents. We were thrilled and stretched by our new lifestyle and adored our wonderful baby boy.

High Stakes

Colin and I got on well, though we were rather like two single parents sharing one home. One of us was always working or leading Buddhist activities while the other took care of Jamie. Certainly we were good friends and loved each other – considerate, cooperative and communicative – but we were not IN love. What passion we shared before Jamie was born had now dwindled. This bothered me more than Colin, a deeply contented and self-contained soul, but it was becoming more and more painful to me. I was only in my early 30s (Colin is 11 years older) and it felt like part of me was dying. We did talk about it, but couldn't find a way to address it.

When Jamie was a toddler, I tried to fill myself by taking on a challenging new Buddhist business project – developing and managing the ethical gift shop, Evolution, which needed an injection of new energy. It was consuming, successful and great fun, but it didn't hit the increasingly big and unsatisfied 'love spot'. I started to wonder about Colin and I remaining together in the future.

"But he's such nice guy!" everyone protested. And they were right. Colin was a lovely man, a wonderful friend and a great dad. He still is. Yet much as I appreciated him, I was increasingly frustrated in our relationship. We just didn't meet on all levels, and a vital part of me remained unexpressed and unfulfilled. But how could I justify wanting to break up with this 'good man'? Surely it wasn't worth wrecking a family over?

Re-Awakening

Aged 33, I was asking myself, "Is this it? Would I never again share my life with a true love that lights up my heart, mind, body and soul? What had happened to the wild, free, passionate young woman that I used to be?"

Then, something happened. A friend introduced me to the liberating dance meditation practice, 5Rhythms. The first time I found myself moving at a class, huge waves of ecstatic joy and release flooded through my body. I was waking up a part of myself that had been asleep for years. It wasn't long before I had thrown myself into regular 5Rhythms practice, and boy oh boy, look out now!

Within six months, I had shed the two stones (28 pounds) of excess weight I had been carrying since I had become a mum. As this comforting, but numbing layer of protection melted away, the real 'me' reemerged and I became alive to my whole self again. I could no longer deny my desire to have a 'proper' relationship again. Before long, I said to Colin that I thought it was only a matter of time before I met someone else. And I did.

Sebastian was a smoldering Spanish guy from the 5Rhythms class. We found ourselves drawn together in dance and then afterwards in the bar. A week or two later, we arranged to meet at a dance party and connected with a kiss. And so began the most intense relationship. A torrent of passion erupted through me; a decade's worth of repressed energy expressing itself all in one go.

Both men knew about each other as I kept everything sensitively honest. Sebastian was understanding, and Colin and I agreed that we would continue living as a family while I explored having a boyfriend 'on the side'. But it was not long before that just did not feel right anymore. As synchronicity would have it, we temporarily moved into a larger house while some repair work was done on our home, so at least Colin and I now had our own bedrooms. When it was time to return, however, I just could not fit myself back into that old mold.

Prompted by me, we decided to separate, made much easier by the availability of a small flat just a few doors away. Colin moved into the flat, and Jamie and I back to the bigger apartment. Jamie could stay with Colin a couple of nights a week and otherwise run freely between homes via our back gardens. Apart from living under two roofs, it seemed nothing would be much different as we continued to co-parent between us.

Emotional Fallout

Although the practical arrangements were uncommonly smooth and Colin and I continued to be extremely calm and friendly with each other, the actual separation was a lot harder than antici-pated. Firstly, and mostly, it was agonizing breaking up Jamie's secure family unit. It just felt wrong at an instinctual, maternal level. The anguish I felt one bedtime as Jamie sobbed, "I want my daddy," was almost too much to bear. Grief and anguish seared through me. Was this too much of a price to pay?

Most of my friends and family were shocked and upset at the news of our split. They posed the question that I had been asking myself for years: couldn't I just sacrifice my personal happiness for the sake of keeping our family together? After all, Colin and I weren't actually falling out. Their understandable concern hit a nerve of doubt, but it did make me realize I was long past that reasoning now, even if I wasn't 100% sure.

Within a month of separation, the emotional impact started to catch up with me. First of all, I hurt my back which laid me up for a few weeks. This meant I had to drop out of yet another new Buddhist business project I had just taken on leading the vegetarian restaurant team. And so I found myself to be a broke, unemployed, single parent in emotional turmoil.

Chapter 20

The Treasure of Truth

Cleaning Up the Mess

After all the moves and changes I felt exhausted, disorientated and insecure. I missed Colin's companionship and my relationship with Sebastian took a different turn now that I was a properly available. It became apparent that this highly charged relationship was severely limited. Sebastian was nowhere near capable of partnering me in the ways that Colin had been. The ensuing fights were just as furious as our loving, and my hysterical reactions shocked me. I really had taken the lid off of my raw emotions in recent months, and there was much to be understood and integrated.

Fortunately, I was well resourced with meditation, 5Rhythms and psycho-synthesis counseling. I also had my amazing friends and family standing by, including Colin who proved once again what a decent guy he is. Knowing 'the only way out is through', I dived deeply into my inner world and embarked upon a healing journey. The grief was immense – perhaps catching up with a lifetime of loss and separation – and many a day I sat before my meditation altar bawling my eyes out.

In one meditation, I 'saw' the grief and loss being experienced by millions of ordinary people throughout the world every day just like me. The immensity of this threatened to tear me apart, but I couldn't hold it at bay. My heart and soul shattered and was replaced by the most exquisite, compassionate solidarity with every single living being in the universe. It was one of those moments that changed me forever.

Finding Myself Again

Somehow, that moment helped me turn a corner, and oh so slowly, I began to reconstruct. I let go of trying to make a partner out of Sebastian and, after a failed job interview back in the 'normal' world, of getting my working life back together just yet. If I was honest, I was still exhausted and didn't know who I was or what I wanted to do next. Crucially, I gave myself permission to stop, and not know, and just BE for a while. There was only one thing I felt capable of doing apart from looking after Jamie, and that was volunteering to teach a lunchtime meditation class at the Buddhist Centre one day a week. That simple oasis of gentle giving proved to be my salvation. While dwelling there, I rebuilt my self-esteem and innocently sowed the seeds of the beautiful, fruitful life that was to follow.

It took me about a year to figure out what next. I didn't push it, just stayed with what felt okay, even if I didn't understand why. As well as the meditation class, I eventually did some consultancy work with a colleague's community development agency a day or two a week. I carried on dancing and hung looser to my Buddhist commitments. That was plenty.

During that time, the inspiration to move to Devon – a rural county in the southwest tip of England – started to murmur within me. I had recently visited Devon's charming market town of Totnes to attend 5Rhythms workshops. Soon afterwards, Susanne (my close friend I'd worked with in Phoenix Housing Co-op) moved to Totnes having also gotten into 5Rhythms and met her new partner there. I was captivated by this 'funky, alternative capital of the UK' and all the fascinating things that were going on.

The countryside in Devon was simply stunning. What a great place for Jamie to grow up. Colin and I at once discovered that there was one place in the whole of the UK apart from London where we would both be happy to live – Devon. This was a vital part of the equation now, as there was no way I wanted to put distance between Jamie and his beloved, hands-on, doting dad. And so when Colin indicated that he was willing to move to Devon too, it was game on.

And so we moved to Totnes, Colin and I living near each other and continuing to co-parent Jamie between us. The first year was demanding, emotional and unsettling, especially for Jamie, but it was also an exhilarating adventure and obviously the right move. A whole new life started to be created there with amazing new friends and colleagues. And it wasn't long until we had more local family living close by as both my sister Katy and Colin's mum and dad relocated to Devon too.

Truth Sets You Free

So, in answer to myself and all my concerned friends and family who once wondered if splitting up with Colin was worth 'wrecking a family' for, it has proved to be a great big "YES!" The family has not been wrecked, it's just that part of it has been dismantled so that a bigger, better family could be reconstructed on stronger, truer foundations. It took me a few years of periodic, low-level guilt to be absolutely convinced of that. But it was finally dispersed a year or so after moving to Devon when Colin and I had a big heart to heart. Enough time had gone by for us to be able to really see that our split had been the right thing, not just for us but for Jamie too.

Okay, we did not manage to stay together in one household, but we have taught Jamie the greater value of honesty, courage and truth in relationships. Each of us has become more ourselves – more expressive, more creative and more fulfilled – and Jamie now has the benefit of both his dad and all his extended family. Plus, crucially, a mum that is alive to herself on all levels.

It is said that we teach more to our kids by example than by any other means. If my choices and actions have helped instill in

Jamie the permission to be fully himself, follow his heart and not to compromise in what he wants from life, then I consider my job as a parent well done. The stakes are sometimes high, but the truth will set you free. We can always rely on that.

Chapter 21

Twin Pearl

A Move to the Country

"Totnes is full of single mothers and hardly any single men," my new friends in Devon told me. "I hope you're not expecting to find a partner here!" But I wasn't moving to Devon to find a partner. After 16 years living in a Buddhist community in London, it was time to move on, and my longing for a rural lifestyle could no longer be ignored. But most importantly of all, Jamie, now nearly seven, deserved a gentler upbringing – more than a city could afford.

Despite the good reasons, however, there was also an element of strange magnetism I couldn't put my finger on. In many ways I was leaving a great situation and jumping into who knows what, but there was a compelling force drawing me on and I had a daring, inexplicable knowledge that this was absolutely the right move. So, one sunny September morning in 2001, I packed my little grey Peugeot car with our belongings, strapped Jamie in the front beside me, and set off for our new life in the country.

My heart was soaring when we got out of the car to stretch our legs at the ancient standing stones of Stonehenge. What an awesome monument to mark the halfway point to Devon! The sky was blue and the stones seemed to be humming with affirmation that we were doing the right thing. We weren't in dirty, frantic, complicated London now. Here was the gateway to a whole new magical realm.

When we arrived, there was a lot to do – a home to find, school for Jamie, money to earn, new friends to make. I was fully occupied and completely excited by the experience of making this beautiful place our home. But by night I was lonely and reeling from all the enormous changes in my life. Sometimes the grief and disorientation were almost unbearable. It would have been so comforting to have someone to share all this with, a manly chest to snuggle into. For a few months I dated halfheartedly, but nothing got off the ground.

I knew that this was because I still had some healing to do, and at last I decided to cooperate with the process. I needed to do what usually has to be done when recovering from one relationship and preparing for another: to stay in the gap for as long as it takes and be with myself for a while. I was overdue to complete some unfinished emotional business: to understand what had happened and why; to let go of hurts and fears; to reassess who I am now; and establish what kind of relationship would be good for me next.

As a meditator I already had an invaluable tool at my disposal. Meditation gives emotional space and opens up a bigger perspective that allows us to face challenges positively. Along with regular chats with insightful friends and family, my meditation practice gave me the resources to navigate my way through the stormy emotional waters.

So did my continued practice of 5Rhythms dance. At my weekly class and in the privacy of my own home, this wonderful form of free expression accessed and gave full voice to the stories and emotions stuck in my body. I danced and roared and stamped and cried (a lot!) and laughed and gave thanks and laid the ghosts to rest. Over the weeks I became clearer, free-er and more peaceful.

In early February, on the pagan day of Imbolc, I attended a sweat lodge held by a lovely local shaman, Carlos Glover, down by the river Dart. In the dark, eerie beauty of a winter forest, we ceremonially heated huge stones in a roaring wooden pyre. Once ready, the hot stones were brought into the lodge one by one and sprinkled with sage water. We sat in a circle inside the lodge, naked and in total darkness, sweating and singing and praying.

It was like being inside a womb of pure spirit. We spoke aloud one at a time, each prayer seeming to come from infinite consciousness and be sent out into the entire universe. My prayer was spontaneous and ardent, "Please help me let go of the past and allow me the time and space I need before I get involved in another relationship."

Making an Invitation

During one of my more contented evenings and inspired by Oriah Mountain Dreamer's poem, *The Invitation*, I did some reflective writing. In a deep, prayerful way, I wrote about what I longed for, the kind of loving partner that would be ideal for me. It was almost sacrilegious to be so honest about what would be utterly wonderful for me. I had never given myself permission to state these things before. But once it was down on paper I found I was moved by the quality of person I was describing in those two dozen short paragraphs. And somehow, having committed my vision to paper, this man began to take on a tangible existence. It was spooky. It was as though I had begun to create a reality, or at least, call a reality towards me.

Having read widely about metaphysical principles since then, I know that this is exactly what is occurring when we make things conscious and decide to move towards them. As Sangharakshita used to say, "It's not so much that man wills, but that will mans." In other words, our will manifests into form not the other way around. We become what we wish for. We create our reality from our thoughts and feelings and expectations.

Now, in my work as a life coach, writing about ideals is an exercise that my clients use with unremittingly powerful results. But back then, I somewhat innocently placed my writings on my meditation shrine and forgot about them. Little did I know that I had planted a seed which would invisibly grow and suddenly blossom into the love of my life.

Chapter 22

Recognizing a Jewel

Meeting My Match

At first I didn't realize I had met him. As far as I was concerned, this 'Pat' guy was just a housemate of a friend I had gotten to know at Jamie's school. Ann and I used to hang out at each other's houses while our boys played together. So my first few meetings with Pat were incidental – brief interactions during a flurry of noisy, stampeding boys needing after school snacks. I was in 'mum mode' and, anyway, I had a background distraction still rolling with one man or another I was half involved with. I wasn't paying attention where it was due. It took me a further couple of months to wake up. And what a wake-up call it was.

Towards the end of April, my much loved gran in Scotland was living out her last days. My sister Katy was giving me bulletins every day and I was waiting for news of her final passing. Life was sharp. My heart was so open. Contrastingly, I was experiencing impossibly crossed wires with a new man I was dating and decided to finish it. The night I told him and left, he fell off his steep garden terrace and was hospitalized with a broken back. I was shocked into further acute awake-ness.

That same week – intuitively picking up on what was about to happen, I'm sure – Sebastian was on the phone from London asking for one last chance. For the first and last time, I said, "No," properly. It was after the sweat lodge prayer and I was crystal clear. Now I was truly free from any involvement whatsoever. I was free to pay attention where it was due.

On the Tuesday, I arrived for a session of Resonance Repatterning with my friend Christina. I had booked the session a week before to help with my relationship with Jamie, but there was something else on the menu. It soon emerged that the key theme I was ready to explore was meeting the right partner. In the session, Christina revealed to me that I held the unconscious belief that, "I could never find a partner that could meet me on all levels." This was a core reason I had been compromising myself in other relationships. She worked with me over two hours to shift this belief, and, three days later...

Pat was covering Ann's child-minding shift that day and we were looking after the boys together in the school yard. It was the first chance Pat and I had to really talk. I told him about my recent breakup. Knowing a bit about me by now, Pat commented that it is very difficult to have a relationship with someone who is not spiritual if you are yourself. I liked him. I liked the way he sprawled wide-legged on some rocks on the edge of the playground, looking like a cowboy from the American Wild West.

Although I didn't know why, I agreed that I might meet Pat for a drink that night. I was feeling incredibly sensitive and antisocial and a pub is the last place I'd go at the best of times, but something led me into the Sea Trout Inn.

The Sea Trout was Pat's regular drinking hole, just a stone's throw from the cottage Jamie and I were living in. I laid aside my puritanical Buddhist prejudices and was pleasantly surprised by the level of meaningful communication happening among the public bar locals. Pat was typically animated and in full flood; "Yah gotta get outta yar head and intta yar heart," he was insisting. He sounded like a cowboy too, or maybe one of those charismatic American preachers.

"A bit full on," I thought to myself, but I was intrigued. And then, suddenly, in the middle of all the passionate discussion, Pat and I paused and gazed intently upon each other. "I... see... you... " he said, slowly and knowingly. "I see you too," I replied with equal gravitas. (Note: this was years before the film *Avatar* came out, where, as the film's theme song *I See You* suggests, they look into one another's souls and say those very words to each other.)

In that moment, we did indeed truly see one another. It was like a lightning flash had struck and lit up the entire vast landscape of who we were. The moment returned to darkness, but the flash revealed something forever. In that moment I realized that I recognized Pat, that I knew him, and with that knowledge was the deepest trust and truest love.

We parted in the car park with us both feeling somewhat stunned. "I lo... lo... lo..." Pat stammered. He seemed to be saying something and stuffing it back into his mouth at the same time. He looked as perplexed as I felt. Was he trying to resist saying that he LOVES me? Surely not?

I went back to the cottage and received the news that Gran had just passed away. Dear Gran. Dear kind, loving, strong, simple, generous, understanding, feisty, affectionate Gran. My spirit couldn't help but elevate to commune with her and God and the afterlife and all of that other indescribable stuff that these words just do not do justice to. Her love and essence were filling the skies and I just had to fly with her for a while.

As if in a dream, I found myself popping into the Sea Trout at Sunday lunchtime to find Pat. It was completely unplanned. All of a sudden I was there inviting him to take a walk on the moors with me. We talked about Gran and meditation. Sitting by a pool, he told me he would have loved to study psychology if he had ever been able to. I told him that psychology had been my main subject at university.

Without thinking about it, I took his hand as we walked back to the car. It was as though a greater force was acting through me. I certainly didn't have the wherewithal to acknowledge what was going on, or make any judgments with my head. I was in the spontaneous and innocent world of my heart alright.

We shared our first kiss in the Sea Trout car park the next evening. I was preparing to go to Gran's funeral later that week.

"Come... Back... To... Me..." Pat said plainly. I'd already explained that I had a few romantic loose ends to tie up and couldn't promise anything. "Take whatever time you need," he replied.

The day before I flew to Scotland, he appeared in the school playground at pick-up time. Pressing a rose quartz crystal into my hand (which signifies love), he wished me well on my trip. Keen interest and support, understanding and freedom; this was a recipe for love. I recognized these qualities from my ideal man list.

It took me another couple of weeks to fully absorb the significance of what was occurring, but in the aftermath of Gran's funeral, it was a simple and inevitable fact that we would be together. "Shall we love each other, then?" Pat had asked after an evening of endless, sublime kissing. I nodded, but it didn't really need an answer.

I had never experienced anything like it. There was no posturing or trying to impress each other and no attempts to hide our less favorable attributes; we were just relaxed and unselfconscious with each other from the very beginning. And there was no question about whether or not we would be together; no push-pull fear of rejection or of being overwhelmed, no insecurity whatsoever. Likewise, there was no great destabilizing intoxication. The feelings were immediate and profound, but our heads were clear and our feet were on the ground. It was so straightforward – complete harmony, complete certainty – and left nothing to negotiate.

Less than a year and a half later, we were married.

Preparing for Divine Relationship

As I was to discover, Pat had also prepared well for the arrival of what he called a 'divine relationship' in his life. A longtime meditator like me, Pat had worked through all the issues raised by previous relationships. He particularly practiced forgiveness (including forgiving himself) and was unusually clear, more so than me, of the sort of relationship backlog that we often carry into future relationships (which we then mess up because we are relating to ghosts instead of the person with us now).

He had also used a specific manifestation meditation to call his vision of a relationship into being. Popularized and taught by Dr. Wayne W. Dyer in the 1990s (having been asked to teach it by the Indian guru, Dr. Pillai), this practice brings together the power of the chakras (energy centers), the voice and creative visualization. I call it the Ah/Om or manifestation meditation.

Most importantly of all, perhaps, Pat adopted an attitude that he referred to as "100% intention with 100% surrender". Although he was very clear about the partner he sought and would not compromise with less, he was also prepared for it not to happen and would be genuinely happy to stay alone should he not find his match.

This is the fine and paradoxical art of being open to one's aspirations and creative possibilities while at the same time being fluid with our expectations. Many people either do not let themselves dream through fear of not succeeding or strangle their dreams by having too much at stake and are therefore too desperate for them to come true.

Often we do not let ourselves aspire by assuming we won't succeed, 'can't have', or corrupt our aspirations into egotistical ambitions by having too much self-worth at stake if they flounder, 'must have'. Either way, it betrays a lack of self-knowledge and self-belief.

When we see ourselves clearly and believe in ourselves, we do not need to push things away or grab things towards us to shore up a hollow sense of ourselves. We can allow things to be what they are, free from what we have invested in them. In this freedom we can experience the natural flow of coming and going, and somewhat magically, all our true needs are satisfied in a state of 'havingness'.

Before my Resonance Repatterning session, I did not believe that I could find a partner who could meet me on all levels. So it was very unlikely that I would attract that sort of relationship. Pat certainly can meet me on all levels. This relationship is easily the most satisfying and stimulating either of us has ever known on the domestic, physical, emotional, intellectual and spiritual levels. It is grounded and it is sacred. We are plumbing depths and scaling heights together that would have been hard to access alone.

A few years after we met, I came across the description of the ideal partner I wrote all that time ago. As Pat and I reread it together, I was filled with a strange, joyful realization. The man who those words described was now nuzzling my neck, sharing my life and my deepest aspirations. It is amazing what we can magnetize into our lives with clear intention and positivity. Now I understand a little more about those compelling forces that brought me to Devon.

Chapter 23

Get Ready for Love Wisdom

Here is my step-by-step guide to finding and attracting your ideal partner into your life. This program has been successfully followed by many of my coaching clients and Get Ready for Love workshop participants.

Step 1 – Relationship Appraisal

Spend some quiet time contemplating what you think and feel about the five questions below. Write down your responses briefly and immediately. Write for yourself, uninhibitedly – you do not have to share this with anyone.

Love, sex and relationship appraisal

a) Who or what is important to you when you consider this area of your life?

b) In what ways are your needs met or not met in this area?

c) How much time per week do you spend on this area of your life?

d) How would you rate this area of your life on a scale of 1 to 10 (10 ideal)?

e) Do you have future aims in this area? If so, what are they?

Relationship History/Map

Sketch out a map of your relationship history with dates and significant events, moves, changes etc. This can just be a list with dates along the side, or if you are moved to write a fuller history, that would be fine.

Step 2 – Ideal Partner Visioning

Somewhere inside we know what kind of relationship or life partner we long for. We have flickers of an ideal that are almost too painfully absent to contemplate. So we don't. We don't think it's possible or that we're good enough for such things. So we shelve our fantasy fragments and settle for less, never believing it could be much different.

But in doing so, we may be missing an opportunity. Our natural ability to imagine and fantasize gives us the potential to make great things happen. Imagination leads the way in how we create our life. Where else does a work of art or a feat of engineering begin but in our imagination? If we can't even imagine where we want to go, we go nowhere, or get blindly swept up with someone else's ideas. Worse still, we drift into a painful nether-world based on our unconscious negative beliefs and imaginings.

To harness the positive creative power of our imagination, we need to be aware of our beliefs about our self and the world. Our beliefs are only ideas picked up and reinforced throughout our lives, a pattern of thinking that helps us feel comfortable. Beliefs have no real substance and yet they strongly influence the creation of our reality.

That is why it is possible to suspend our habitual beliefs and reach somewhere else in our imagination. We can loosen our beliefs about what is possible, and strengthen our positive tone. It is excellent practice to give our beliefs a good stretch every now and then. We can play with them, see them for what they are, show them who is boss.

The Ideal Relationship Visioning exercise uses these principles. It is a chance to play at stretching our ideas about how our life could be towards something utterly amazing. We suspend disbelief and allow ourselves to reach way into perfection. It doesn't matter if we don't think we can ever achieve this kind of partnership. In the process of the exercise we free ourselves up and reveal what really moves us.

We will deal with how we make things real later. For now, forget the how and shoot for the stars. Have a go...

Take a leap of imagination into a life with a romantic partnership that is totally wonderful and ideal for you. What would your life together be like if everything about your relationship was totally fantastic and in line with your deepest values?

In this scenario, you cannot fail; you have everything you could possibly hope for. Let rip. Let your soul sing. It is so exhilarating to just give yourself permission, to have a real stretch. This is about what you would love to be true, not what you believe is achievable. Suspend all ideas about what is possible and go for it.

Describe your ideal relationship life vividly using all your senses. How would the world seem in the midst of this great love? How would you, your partner and the environment you are in look, smell, taste and feel? Make it as luscious and colorful and as over the top as you like.

Use entirely positive language – describe what you want, not what you don't want. For example, you may want your partner to "only have eyes for me, making me feel like the most beautiful and desirable woman in the world" (rather than stating that he doesn't have a roving eye for other women).

If you don't know the exact form of what you want – e.g. how your love would look – describe the essence instead. For example, describe how you are totally attracted to your partner and love every physical attribute they have. On the other hand, if you do have a strong preference – e.g. for a dark haired partner – feel free to state that clearly.

You may discover that you want things from an ideal partner that seem contradictory. For example, you may want to feel very secure and wanted, and at the same have the space to be free and independent. Perhaps in your experience so far you have only had relationships where your partner was either: a) doting and attentive but cramped your style; b) gave you plenty of space but didn't seem to put you at the center of his life enough. In this visioning, make sure you have your 'cake and eat it', even if you can't imagine how it could be because you've never experienced both those qualities simultaneously before.

Write in the present tense as though it is all actually happening now, e.g. "I wake in the morning next to my beloved soul mate..." Create a reality and step inside it.

Some questions to consider:

a) What kind of relationship would you have? What interests would you share? How would you be spending your time together and apart? Where would you be? How would you live? Who else, if any, would be around you? How would you express yourself and communicate with each other?

b) Can you make your daydream bigger and better? Be bold.

c) What is your ideal partner like? What are they interested in? How do they spend their time? What are they like physically, mentally, emotionally, spiritually? If you don't know clearly, describe the qualities of this person and what it is like being around these qualities. Don't be shy about your tastes and desires and secret hopes – this is your dream, you can have whatever you like.

d) How do you feel about each other? How do you feel being with this special person? How do they regard you, and how do they express this?

A bit stuck?

Try creating a picture or collage of your ideal partner/ partnership. Use big paper, words, color, cut up magazines, anything that inspires you.

If you have a lot of resistance, objections and cynical comments in your head, write them down. Leave them aside to deal with later. If they persist, turn the negative objections upside down into positive affirmations and write them out, e.g. "I'll never find the man of my dreams" becomes "I am delighted at how easily I have found my perfect match."

If a lot of unresolved feelings come to the surface during this part of the exercise, you may wish to seek some extra support from a counselor or therapist, or try some self-help like EFT (Emotional Freedom Technique).

Step 3 – Practical Steps

Bringing your dream to earth

Now it is time to look again at the changes you would love to manifest in your life and hatch practical plans, ideas and strategies to help make it happen. Remember this is a process, with immediate, intermediate, and long-term steps and events that you can manage one at a time.

Stay positive

Plans work best when you keep the language positive (i.e. describing what you want, not what you don't want).

Think SMART

Plans also work best when they are **S**pecific, **M**easurable, **A**chievable, **R**ewarded, and **T**ime-framed. Stay bold and optimistic, but be realistic and practical.

Be specific and detailed

Drawing from your visioning, begin by defining what you *really* want in each area of your life (i.e. in day-to-day reality). When would you like this to happen by? What needs to occur before it could happen? What actions can you take? Answer these questions:

Exactly **what** do you want?
When do you want to achieve it by?
How will you achieve it? Think of as many options as you can.
How long will this take?
What **steps** can you take along the way?

Recognize and reward your progress

What **rewards and encouragement** will you give yourself as you achieve each step?

How will you **recognize** that you have achieved each step and made the changes? Imagine how things will **look, feel and sound**.

Support your changes

Ask yourself who or what will support you while you go through this process. Do you need to ask family or friends for support (time, understanding, space)? Do you need some other resources like a book or a club or some specific information? Make a clear list of these and note beside each how and when you will set this support up.

Plan on paper

Think of the steps you are taking and make a vision map.

Plot 'now' on the left and a time (e.g. May – single) and goal to aim towards (e.g. September – in a relationship) on the right. Draw a circle around each of them.

Draw a number of circles leading from left to right, filling the page, like a spread of stepping stones across a river.

In the middle of the circles, write in the steps, activities and events that need to happen from left to right based on all the ideas you have generated above. (To the left, write in the earlier steps that need to happen first, and to the right, the later steps.)

This gives you a visual map of the stepping stones from where you are now to where you want to be.

Writing up and reinforcing your plan

Finally, rewrite your ideas towards your aspiration (including all the details you've generated) using the present tense, i.e. as though it is really happening. The present tense speaks to your unconscious mind. To reinforce your aspirations in your conscious mind, practice reading through your write-up once a day.

An example

"I have established my ideal love partnership by September. I achieved this by having some relationship coaching in April and May.

This resourced me to review my aims, envision my ideal partnership, learn techniques and make clear plans which I successfully followed throughout the summer. It felt great to be confident and inspired.

Having practiced the Ah/Om manifestation meditation for 10 minutes every morning and evening from June, I felt galvanized to pursue online dating and other 'meet my partner' ideas.

When I made my first date, I rewarded my boldness by buying a new outfit and felt great. After meeting a few people, I quickly and easily met someone very special.

Taking things at a pace I felt comfortable with and supported by reporting back to my best friend over coffee every week, I got to know my new date and discovered we were an ideal match.

I was reassured to know I could melt away concerns or worries about being with a partner again with EFT tapping.

In August we decided to go on holiday together in September. It was a dream come true, and such a reward for my trust and willingness to open to relationship again."

Step 4 – Appreciating Yourself

It is so important to remember what we have to give in relationship, as well as what we want. Sometimes we can become so fixed on our ideal partner 'shopping list' that we forget about what qualities we offer. In fact, we rarely appreciate ourselves and our gifts enough. This simple exercise remedies that, putting us in the energy of giving rather than wanting – which is hugely more attractive and magnetic to potential new partners.

50 Reasons Why I Make a Wonderful Partner

Write a list of AT LEAST 50 reasons why you make a wonderful partner.

List all your qualities, interests, abilities in relationships – however big or small – the things that make you YOU.

For example:

I am affectionate
I am a great cook
I love dogs
I am emotionally intelligent

Step 5 – Create a Love Altar

Find a place in your home where you can create a love altar, in a corner of your bedroom or on a table in the conservatory (sunroom), for example. Gather a few objects or images that inspire you about love and place them together and perhaps add a candle or some flowers.

Put your Ideal Relationship Visioning and your other writing, reflections and drawings on the altar so you can easily look at them and read them.

Spend a few minutes every day sitting by your love altar, rereading your ideal visioning and reaffirming your intentions for a wonderful relationship to come into your life. You can also practice the following manifestation meditation by your love altar.

Step Six – Manifestation Magic

Ah Om Manifestation Meditation

The Ah and Om manifestation meditation is a powerful manifestation practice that spiritual teacher Dr. Wayne W. Dyer taught widely in the 1990s (having been requested to do so by the meditation's channel, Indian sage, Dr. Pillai). The meditation is used to open up and energize the metaphysical power of asking for and receiving that which we wish to draw into our life.

The meditation combines the power of the mind, the body and the voice into a singular, intentional energy. We 'put out' this energy, and then we let go and allow ourselves to receive.

It can be used to draw to us physical things (like cars, houses), positive relationships, states of emotional and mental well-being, as well as health, money, clients and jobs. It is very powerful and effective for manifesting ideal love relationships.

We can choose to energize the same request over and over again each time we do the meditation, or we can change our request each time we do it as appropriate. For the purpose of manifesting your ideal partner, focus on this subject daily for the best results. (This is what Pat did for a few months before he met me.)

The meditation can be done collectively as well as on our own. It is very powerful to join with others on a collective purpose using this meditation, or done collectively even if everyone is focusing on individual and different desired outcomes.

It is a short (20 minutes x 2) and powerful practice that can be done as part of a daily routine, and/or employed for specific projects. It can also be done to open and close group meetings and ceremonies.

The Ah part of the meditation is best done earlier, e.g. first thing in the morning, and the OM part later, e.g. last thing in the evening. Both parts are important, the asking and the receiving.

The Ah is a 'seed' sound syllable that represents the out breath – birth, life, bliss, and awakening. It sends energy out to the universe.

The Om is a 'seed' sound syllable that represents the in breath – receptivity, gratitude and surrender. It receives energy from the universe.

How to practice:

1. First choose one thing to focus on – e.g. the desire to find and share life with your ideal love match.

2. Being as specific as you can, turn this need or desire into a positive affirmation, asserting that you already have this thing – e.g. I share my life with the most beautiful and perfect soul-mate life partner.

3. Repeat this silently in your mind, over and over again – e.g. "I have a beautiful, perfect partner," "I have a beautiful, perfect partner." Imagine scenarios of your life together and live out all the good feelings you have sharing your life and dreams with your ideal partner.

4. Think of/visualize/feel/get a sense of the energy in your base chakra (at the genital area or perineum). Imagine drawing up this energy, up through your sacral chakra (below the belly button), up through your solar plexus chakra, up through your heart chakra, up through your throat chakra, and up to your third eye chakra (in the middle of the forehead just above the eyes).

5. Imagine the energy you are drawing up from your base chakra and through the other chakras is streaming out of your third eye chakra. It streams out of the third eye chakra, out into the universe, powerfully and unreservedly. All your body energy is streaming up and out of this chakra, the visioning chakra. It rolls on and on endlessly.

6. Keep mentally reciting the affirmation. At the same time, keep rolling the energy up through your chakras and out through the third eye chakra. Now add the third element, your voice chanting 'Ah'.

7. Chant the syllable 'Ah' out loud with the out breath. Pause during the in breath, then chant 'Ah' again at the same pitch. Keep repeating the 'Ah' with the out breath. Keep the chanting going for 20 minutes, allowing the voice to come and go in force as feels appropriate. Keep reciting the affirmation and gushing out the energy from the chakras as you do so.

8. Later on, perhaps at the other end of the day before bed, sit down quietly again. Remember what you chanted Ah for earlier, your 100% intention. Allow yourself to soften and feel receptive to whatever good may come your way.

9. Now chant 'Om' for 20 minutes with the out breath. As you chant, let go of all attachment, all 'must have', in relation to what you chanted Ah for. Completely surrender to trusting that whatever will be will be. This is your 100% surrender.

10. Instead, as you continue to chant Om, focus on all the blessings you already have in your life, however big or small. Allow yourself to feel appreciation for all you already have – especially all the love and good relationships you already have. This cultivates a state of 'havingness' which makes you magnetic to having and receiving even more.

Chapter 24

Every Pearl Is Perfect

A Cornishman with Attitude

The extraordinary thing about connecting with Pat is that he was *nothing* like anyone I had been hanging out with in decades. For a start, his favorite place to socialize was the pub – something that was completely alien to me being a teetotaling ordained Buddhist. It wasn't just the drinking that made us an unlikely couple, however; it was also his smoking, meat eating and TV watching.

Much as I had been massively sensitized to avoid all that, in fact I'd taken *vows* against most of it and would normally find those behaviors off-putting, in Pat's case I didn't seem to notice. This is a bit of an odd phenomenon to describe, but I guess it was a matter of connecting with Pat's true being so profoundly and finding him so alluring at that deep level that those relatively superficial things just didn't register.

In fact I have now come to recognize that these differences between us have been part of the magic of our relationship and one of my greatest lessons. Falling in love with a man who, in spiritual circles, is considered to behave so 'blasphemously' has been an excellent antidote to any spiritual preciousness I was carrying. It helped me drop any hoity-toity idea of what is proper and 'spiritual' – the right thing to eat, the right thing to wear, the right thing to say – and recognize that true spirituality comes in many guises.

So how come I found this beer swilling, cigarette puffing, TV watching Cornishman so compelling? The truth is, Pat is one of the most profoundly spiritually evolved people I have ever known, and I must have intuitively sensed that right away, despite appearances.

He is a trickster, a holy fool, often misunderstood and misjudged, but those who see and love him, really see and love something extraordinary. For a start, although he can appear fierce, impatient and provocative (a redheaded, Aries/Dragon-born, Cornishman with attitude), Pat loves powerfully and unconditionally and carries no judgment of others. His challenges are a form of play and a call for whoever he is talking with to wake up to themselves. Most unusually, however, he is not doing it for any personal gratification – to score a point or make him feel good – and is not attached to any particular outcome. In fact, most often his playful prods are involuntary, a kind of automatic truth-seeking reflex. He calls it his curse, but of course it is his gift too.

True Love Cuts Deep

Finding the right partner is a priority among many of my coaching clients. I have had the great joy of assisting many through to that magical moment of meeting someone amazing; the 'wow' moment when all the soul work pays off. I have also had the fulfillment of then supporting the same person navigating the deepening waters of relationship once it is established (sometimes coaching the couple together).

The job is not done when we finally meet our match. Not surprisingly, whatever personal issues we each carry about relationship reemerge big time once the relationship is under way. It is all there to be made conscious and explored and resolved should we choose to, and actually, being with someone throws it all up into stark, potent reality.

There is something about a sexual love relationship that touches us more deeply than anything else. It stirs up our deepest and darkest as well as our most brilliant and best. This is something I was reassuring a newly lovesick client about. "A fine mess you've got me into, Stanley" she titled her e-mail. "Help, I can't eat, work, sleep!" she exclaimed.

Of course, I hadn't got her into anything. She had called it all up herself, and after three months of diligent intention and attention, had manifested the most incredible match imaginable. She found 'Him'! This is a person with so much sorted, so much going for her. Yet, she has only just opened a door to a whole new rich and vulnerable dimension of herself by finally opening to deep relationship.

This is something I can relate to. Before meeting Pat, I had spent the best part of 20 years living semi-monastically in a Buddhist community. Our romantic relationships were conducted peripherally and we were encouraged to live and work independently in order to dedicate ourselves to our spiritual practice.

Deep down I intuitively knew that my greatest spiritual growth opportunity was destined to come from entering deeply into a loving partnership with a man. And I was right. What was in store for me upon meeting Pat was a spiritual revolution. It also prompted the discovery of my true vocation in Thrivecraft, and has been a most fruitful and creative time of my life.

You Know Best

You know best. You do! It was only once I started learning from this wonderful, maverick, not-what-you-expect-from-a-spiritual guy 'Holy Cornishman' that I started to really take this in for myself that I know best. That and the fact that I am 'good enough' just the way I am!

Maybe you have been inspired by spiritual growth, self-help and personal development for some time, perhaps you are even a coach, counselor, teacher or caring professional yourself. You have a pile of books that have guided you to meet the right partner, practice meditation and attract abundance. You have attended workshops, watched videos, taken online courses and gained qualifications. You have put some amazing things into place in your life and connected with some lovely like-minded people along the way.

And it has been great. Fantastic stuff, life is so much better for it. However, there is still a nagging feeling that you could do better, that you are not good enough or doing it right. Maybe you are not practicing your meditation often enough, or earning enough money from your coaching practice, or managing to stick to those healthy foods that you know do you so much good. And even though you are well versed in the principle that love triumphs fear – and so should know better – you are still not free of those low-level, creeping doubts, worries and fears.

Believe me, you are not alone. I know thousands of people just like you who share this paradox – terrific, inspiring, positive people who are doing fantastic things in their professional and personal lives, but still give themselves a hard time – myself included very occasionally. I was pondering this phenomenon when I suddenly got it. We believe that we are supposed to learn lessons and continually 'improve' ourselves, when actually, we don't need to work at changing a thing. Not really, at least, not with that attitude. It is far more important that we realize that we are already perfect, just the way we are.

Perfect Just the Way You Are

But aren't we supposed to be ridding ourselves of ego, healing our inner child and forgiving those who have wronged us? Our books and teachings are full of instructions on the art of waking up, healing wounds, letting go and moving on. And the whole coaching model is about getting from where you are now to where you want to be.

However, if you look deeply into the spiritual essence of any edict that really works, you will see there is only one true starting point – LOVE YOURSELF JUST THE WAY YOU ARE. It is in accepting yourself just the way you are, first and foremost, that real and lasting positive change is catalyzed. That is the transformational power of love. This is changeless change – or at least, effortless, graceful, natural change.

When I first met Pat, he shared with me the story of a profound experience he'd had in meditation. He was taken on a visionary journey by an angelic figure that showed him a scene where nearly everyone on earth was "walking away from themselves".

Ironically, the people who were walking away from themselves the most were the strivers and spiritual seekers. In their earnest and often self-critical drive to reach greater consciousness, they were the very ones who were estranging themselves the most from their true nature.

The paradoxical thing is that, ultimately, there is nowhere to go and nothing to change! There are many tales of enlightened saints who, when they awaken, simply laugh and laugh and laugh. Perfection was right there in front of their noses all along. Everything is perfect! They are perfect! The world is perfect!

Chapter 25

Missing the Treasure

A Ceremony on a Hill

The friendly old Scottish hotel on the banks of a tree-lined river had seen its best, but it didn't matter. We were glad to have found somewhere to stay and it meant there weren't many people around. After a pleasant dinner, we sat in a corner of the big, airy, darkening lounge all by ourselves, talking intently, still so much to learn about each other. Pat was about to share with me one of the most pivotal experiences of his life.

It was a fair May in the Scottish Highlands, quiet before the main tourist season, yet light until nearly bedtime. Peaceful and awe-inspiring, the distant mountains were reassuring, while nearby Loch Tay hummed silently, reminding us of our own vast, inky depths.

Pat and I had taken this trip to Scotland for my dear gran's ash scattering ceremony. We had only known each other for six weeks, but it was obvious Pat should come with me, even though it meant him stepping directly into the heart of the family. My sister, Katy, felt this too, instinctively inviting Pat to also take a handful of Gran's ashes and scatter them, despite never having met him before.

High among the hills overlooking a favorite loch, a dozen of us gathered in a circle. We had chosen this spot because Gran loved her day trips to the area and said she felt "close to God" out in the countryside. Gazing out over the distant loch with small clouds of ash still wafting around us, we spontaneously broke into a Scottish lament. Pat – moved to the core by the haunting song, the glorious vista and the significance of the occasion – had, in that one ceremonial act, definitively become a full member of the family.

It seemed so right. After all, Pat and I had begun our relationship on the very night that Gran passed over. I felt her with me then, blessing my new union from the other side, and I felt her now, up there in the hills above Loch Lomond in her final resting place. For me, Pat and Gran will always be entwined in my heart: both fiery spirits, full of fun, life-force and affection; both so generous with their natural, earthy wisdom; and both havens of love, support and guidance in my life.

Walking Away from Themselves

The day after the ceremony, Pat and I set off to explore for a few days before driving back to Devon. Sitting in the hotel lounge that first evening, naturally dropping into deeper and deeper intimacy, Pat gave me a glimpse into the most hidden chambers of his soul. What I saw in there told me a great deal about the man I was falling in love with, stirring and haunting my spiritual imagination, as it has done to this day.

Pat described a vision he had recently experienced in meditation. He was almost destitute at the time, having just broken up from his relationship (his third marriage in so many decades) which also forced the close of their joint business – the same ruining conclusion as wife number two. Having persuaded friends to put him up in their shared house on an organic farm, he took refuge in their only space: a windowless loft, sleeping on a mattress on the floor.

Directionless, loveless, jobless, and penniless, Pat entered into a period of intense monk-like contemplation, or "cycling" as he called it. Spending much time alone, and being answerable to no one, he simply followed his natural inclination to meditate, commune with spiritual guidance, read, sleep, eat, drink and socialize in whatever random pattern arose throughout the days and nights.

One morning, he woke feeling especially drawn into meditation. Feeling he wanted to gain some higher perspective, he visualized himself ascending stairs while dropping deeper and deeper into trance. Eventually, he found himself sitting on the edge of a wooden jetty, feet dangling over a great sparkling lake that spread out before him. A wise, benign spiritual being was sitting beside him.

Gazing softly at the expansive lake, Pat watched scene upon scene appear in the water. He saw warring countries, he saw friends at odds with each other, and he saw spiritual seekers trying to find themselves. And in every case, his spiritual companion telepathically communicated the same message – "They are walking away from themselves."

His wise guide showed him that the people who were walking away from themselves the most were, in fact, the spiritual seekers; striving to find themselves yet looking in the wrong place. They were trying to 'go somewhere', yet they need only stop and be where they were. They were looking for something outside of themselves that could only be found within.

In those few minutes, Pat's world turned upside down and inside out. He was hit with the thunderous realization that: "Nothing matters and we need do nothing." Reeling from this experience, he tried to conclude the meditation, but it was not finished with him. As the vision faded, a tsunami of pure spiritual energy poured towards him, engulfing him and smashing his old perspective to pieces.

Pat didn't know what to do with himself. He came downstairs to discover he'd left some fish fingers (fish sticks) in the deep fat fryer which were now blown up like pufferfish. "The meaning of life is fish fingers," he mumbled to himself like a mad man. Getting hold of his friend Ann (the child-minder friend who had orchestrated our meeting) on the phone, her advice to him was to go outside and walk barefoot on the grass. It was something, but it wasn't enough.

Still desperate for some support and unable to contact his spiritual mentor and Reiki instructor, Mickey, Pat went to the pub. His drinking mates thought he was totally bonkers and tried to shut him up. Pat now wonders if the experience was not properly absorbed because he took himself into an environment where nobody would even remotely understand what he was on about. However, he did what he did and it was what it was – after all, nothing really matters!

A Spiritual Seeker

One thing was for sure, Pat had just had one of the biggest insights of his life. As he recounted the tale to me, sitting in that hotel lounge, the hairs on the back of my neck stood up. I could feel the power and truth of it and, having been an ardent 'spiritual seeker' within the Triratna for the last 18 years, felt shocked yet intrigued to consider that maybe he and his spirit guide had a point!

I had indeed been 'striving' all those years – looking, searching and seeking – to find enlightenment. After all, the Buddha's dying words were reputedly, "With mindfulness, strive on!" And yes, I had turned within, practiced meditation daily and learned a great deal about myself. However, there was still an attitude of (what Pat calls) 'over-there-ness' subtly inherent in my spiritual quest.

My experience of total immersion in the Triratna was stimulating, educational and insightful, but it also had limitations. It seems to me that there is inevitably some form of institutionalized ideology at work within a spiritual community, even a community that professes the dangers of institutionalized ideology, as ours did. (Maybe even *particularly* when it does; we can be fooled into thinking we are immune from it.)

Sure, we were all taught that we needed to break free of the fetter of getting attached to ideology, rules and practices – and even Buddhism itself – as ends in themselves, rather than simply using them as practical means to an end, but it is so easy to become blind to unconscious, creeping institutionalization when your whole world consists of that institution, as it did to us.

We were all familiar with the Buddha's analogy that once you cross the river of Samsara (suffering) in the boat of the Dharma (spiritual practice) you didn't need to take the boat with you onto the other shore. It had done its job and you could let it go. However, in my experience, it was easy to accidentally hang onto the boat. Or worse than this, it was possible to get so fixated on your boat that you forgot you were on a journey to the other shore at all!

One of the main limiting beliefs I unconsciously created during the time I was in Triratna was a lack of faith in my individual spiritual discernment, my intuition and inner wisdom. This was a bit ironic considering that we were all supposed to be committed to achieving our own enlightenment.

I think this was an accidental consequence of Triratna's emphasis on spiritual friendship. Running everything past our spiritual friends, we were encouraged to open ourselves up to feedback on every matter. This was well intentioned and very helpful and growth-inducing up to a point, but ultimately led to me not having true belief in myself. It was also implied that we should be suspicious of our 'intuition'; that it was probably just our ego in disguise, duping us into thinking we were being wise. Nothing could be trusted unless we had checked it out with our spiritual friends for validation.

During the time I was deciding to leave my community in London for fresh pastures in Devon, I had a vivid dream. The beautifully restored former Victorian fire station that housed the London Buddhist Centre was being flattened. Watching the epicenter of the Triratna's flagship urban village being inexplicably and completely demolished, I felt very sad and disorientated, but also strangely liberated.

My Buddhist friends in London were extremely dubious about my urge to move to Devon. Why would I move out of the most dynamic center in the movement to live away from my spiritual friends in Totnes? Sure, there were spiritual seekers in Devon, but not any of my brothers and sisters in the Dharma. Sangharakshita had warned us about spiritual liberalism. 'Shopping around' different spiritual influences was not deemed as effective as committing yourself to one clear path with one unified community.

In retrospect, that open-ness to all spiritual traditions was exactly the kind of culture that was attracting me to Totnes, but at the time, I couldn't answer my spiritual friends in London. I just knew I had to make the move. Fortunately, for once I listened to my inner promptings over the opinions of my friends and made the move.

Chapter 26

Opening the Oyster

Fully Embracing Universal Wisdom

One of the things that happened when I moved to Devon was that my inner life became much more powerful. Quieted by the beautiful and peaceful countryside and deepened by my practice of 5Rhythms dance and nature-based wisdoms like Shamanism, I developed a more receptive relationship with spirituality.

I was no longer constantly referring to friends for validation or to feedback from my workmates or communards and was thrown back on my own experience. Moving to a new place, shedding my old identity and encountering rich new stimulation sparked a spiritual reinvigoration within me. I entered one of the most mystical phases of my life so far and was propelled into months of visionary experience.

By the autumn of 2002, I had been living in Devon for a year. It was beginning to dawn on me that I was outgrowing my Triratna family like a young adult outgrows the parental home. When I left London I had no intention of resigning my ordination, but a year later with my new life blossoming, I felt curtailed by my spiritual identity as a member of the Order. In fact I felt curtailed by my spiritual identity as a 'Buddhist' altogether.

By now I had met a wonderful man, my soul mate, Pat. Meeting him opened up my spiritual perspective enormously. As well as being a meditator like me, he was widely read and realized, and his inspiration came from many different sources. He introduced me to contemporary teachers like Abraham-Hicks and traditional streams of wisdom like mystical Christianity and Christ Consciousness; teachings that I knew nothing about because I had been exclusively immersed in Buddhism for the best part of 20 years.

One of Pat's influences was ascension and channeling; something I had never come across during my years of intensive Buddhist focus, yet found intriguing and exhilarating. This body of spiritual wisdom seemed to include a more 'feminine' approach to awakening – inviting receptivity to and the allowing of external spiritual forces to move through you, in contrast to my previous Buddhist striving and self-conquering 'masculine' paradigm.

Our housewarming party was the unanticipated trigger for me to actually resign my ordination. Drawing from all the spiritual influences that inspired me at the time, I wove together and led a ceremony that felt just right for the occasion. But it didn't feel right to be creating and guiding a composite, multi-faith, universal ceremony while being an ordained Buddhist. Being 'just' a Buddhist didn't fit me anymore. It didn't ring true. I felt the same way about leading meditation classes. For a while, my new friends had been asking me to teach them meditation, but something was blocking me from doing so.

Eventually I realized that I didn't want to be leading a class as a representative of a Buddhist Order, or any religious community for that matter. In the end, it was a very clean, simple and sudden decision to resign my ordination. I woke up one morning soon after the housewarming ceremony and absolutely knew that I no longer wanted to be part of the Order. There was no fuss, no negative emotion and no drama, only a deep knowing that it was time to move on, along with enormous gratitude for all that I had experienced in Triratna.

The first thing to do was to talk to my preceptor, Sanghadevi, and let her know. She at first asked me to take six weeks to think about it and talk to my spiritual friends and mentors. However, there was no need. I phoned her back the next day and confirmed that I was sure. And so in November 2002, nine years after my ordination at the Dhanakosa Scottish retreat center, I gracefully resigned from Triratna.

Visitations

Lying in bed with Pat the night after my resignation was accepted, I had a vision of my energy being liberated from a small net of light in the cosmos – the closed circuit of the Triratna – and released to flow freely again along the infinite energy network of the Universe.

As Pat held his healing hands over me, it seemed like a demon-like entity suddenly shot from my solar plexus and hurtled out of me into outer space. I let out a yell of surprise, my body jerking like I had just had an electric shock from a resuscitation team. I gasped as I guessed I had been host to this entity during my time in the Triratna. It was small, but definitely had a dark energy. I was shocked to learn an entity had been there at all, let alone one that was less than loving.

However, there were mostly very positive and pleasant visitations around that time. One night, when I was concerned about whether we had enough money, a 10-foot angel with golden coins pouring endlessly from his pockets appeared in the corner of our bedroom. The message was reassuring: "You will always have plenty of money." Curiously enough, in the next few days, I had an unexpected financial windfall and came upon a fantastic new training course that I wanted to do which was grant funded and therefore free of charge.

The angel appeared around the same time that Pat had a visitation from my dad. Dad, who passed away 20 years ago in 1982, often made his otherworldly presence felt these days. It seemed he was handing over guidance and wisdom about my welfare to Pat. On this occasion, Dad simply whispered the word "providence" to him. Not knowing what it meant, we had to look up the word providence in the dictionary the next day. We were glad to glean that Dad was trying to reassure us that we would always be provided for as the definition was "God's Divine provision". Dad, too, was answering my concerns about money.

The old farmhouse where I now lived with Pat was a spooky place, though not scary. Several of us all saw the same ghosts: including an old man with a rope tying his coat together near the back bedroom and an anxious old woman in the corner of the living room. (She wasn't at all sure about us being there, though settled down when we chatted with her and told her we meant no harm.) A medium friend of ours said the farm cottage was a psychic junction, with lots of spirits and supernatural activity coinciding there.

A common phenomenon for me at the farm was unintentionally and telepathically blowing up electrical light bulbs. Sometimes all I needed to do was walk past one and it would shatter explosively for no reason. Friends have since suggested that sometimes our energy affects inanimate objects like this, especially electrical equipment. My psychic energy certainly seemed very powerful and overflowing at the time, so maybe I was too much for the light circuit!

The energy in the farmhouse was eventually completely changed in the course of running meditation classes, life coaching sessions and Thrivecraft groups there. This cleanse began with the housewarming ceremony soon after I moved in – involving chanting and the wafting of sage smoke, or smudging – and finished with a shamanic drumming circle just before we moved out.

The Birth of Thrivecraft

As part of 'meeting on all levels', Pat and I found we had a wealth of different but complementary knowledge and experience to share and an enormous fusion of inspiration occurred between us. We were together day and night, seven days a week during those first months of our relationship. In fact, this continued for our first five years with the exception of two weekends where I was away from Devon. It was a bit like being on continuous intensive retreat together. There was much spiritual catalyzing going on and it was a very powerful time.

Before long, Pat and I realized that we wanted to put out a body of work together, something that captured all this wisdom, experience and practice in a form that was beneficial to others. We knew that we had an offering to give, but what was it, how could we package it? Fortunately, one of our friends said, "It sounds like you could be life coaches." We hadn't heard of life coaching, but we were interested in what our friend described to us. The more we found out about this exciting new profession making its way to the UK from the US, the surer we were that life coaching could indeed be just the vehicle for us.

My spiritual perspective had always been broad and eclectic, even as a Buddhist. I could see how all the world religions, philosophies and psychologies were trying to make sense of the same universal wisdom and make it relevant within different times and cultures. In addition, my instinct was to be out in the wider community, bringing meditation and spiritual teaching to all sorts of people in all sorts of situations, regardless of their religious orientation. I had a growing feeling that I didn't just want to be teaching Buddhism to Buddhists. By the end of my time in London, I had already hatched the idea of setting up a personal development consultancy that would be accessible to non-Buddhists. And now, a few years later in Devon, the form that 'consultancy' could take was clearer.

It made sense for at least one of us to train as a life coach and so I did some research into two or three good courses that were available. I contacted Newcastle College distance learning because Pat knew they ran a business coaching course, and miraculously, the college had just opened applications to their first ever life coaching course and were currently enrolling. Even more miraculously, they were offering the course free of charge. Amazing! I took that as an immense "YES!" from the universe and dived in.

Pat preferred to study informally, so it was only I who officially took the course while sharing my learning and assignments with him as I went along. We were raring to go, with so much over-spilling from us to give to others. As a Buddhist Order Member, I had already been coaching, mentoring and teaching for many years, and so, before I had completed the course, we got on with setting up our new practice.

But what should we call it? I had been running my own community development consultancy for a couple of years and had been musing on the name 'Thrive'. Then Pat suggested an interesting addition. How about we also use the word 'craft' to emphasize the practical/how-to aspect of what we had to offer? And so, on 1st May 2003, our inspirational coaching practice was born – Thrivecraft.

Chapter 27

Wisdom in a Crisis

Calling in a Guide

Something that I was beginning to learn during my spiritual renaissance with Pat is that it is possible to access the most powerful, loving and wise help, advice and guidance – seemingly out of nowhere – and that it is very simple to do. Like many of life's natural treasures, this precious resource is right in front of our noses, absolutely free of charge and almost effortless to tap into. And yet relatively few of us are aware of its existence, or how to go about it.

Even someone steeped in spiritual practice like me can pass by this wonderful source of personal spiritual guidance. Sensing that I would have a particular affinity with it, Pat introduced me to the idea of channeling spiritual guidance when we first met in 2002, but it was some years later before I engaged with it purposefully.

Dragging My Feet

My spiritual education had been almost entirely Buddhist in my 20s and 30s, so I had never really heard of channeling or spiritual guidance before I met Pat, apart from the kind of thing mediums do to speak to the dead. Although it had been satisfying and sometimes thrilling being so deeply and thoroughly schooled in Buddhism, when I learned about these other spiritual perspectives, it was even more fulfilling and exciting. I entered into a powerful and liberating further spiritual awakening.

Pat had studied many metaphysical books in depth including *A Course in Miracles*, *Conversations with God*, the early work of

Abraham-Hicks and was also well read in Ascension and Channeling. He had also participated in Arnold Patent's Celebration of Abundance Workshops and support groups.

When he shared them with me, I found these approaches totally refreshing, giving context to much of what I had sensed intuitively, but never had the conceptual framework to explore or articulate. They resonated with much of Buddhism, but expanded my range of expression and gave validation to the more mystical side of me, something that had been incidentally suppressed by the Triratna framework I had held to for so many years.

Meeting Pat was powerful enough in terms of the unparalleled mind, body and spirit connection we were experiencing together, but taking the lid off my spiritual container with these new possibilities was absolutely revolutionary.

It was probably about five more years before I decided to attempt to connect with a defined, recognizable personal spiritual guide. By this time, I was already informally channeling guidance via my writing, and had had a dalliance with a guide I had casually called upon to help me write a book, but I didn't really know what I was doing.

Introducing Clarion

Then one afternoon, I came across a copy of the book *Opening to Channel* by Sanaya Roman and Duane Packer at a friend's house-clearance sale. Pat had a copy at home as well as several more books by them, but *Opening to Channel* was the one that he had often mentioned as he thought I would particularly enjoy it. Finally, I took notice. This copy at the sale had a strong magnetism and I knew that I had to have it. It seemed to be a message from the Universe that this was my time.

Having read *Opening to Channel* with great interest, I was soon ready to conduct my 'ceremony of welcome' as instructed to invite a guide to make contact with me. In the process, I learned a few important things about the best way to connect with a guide. One was that it is good to ask to connect with our highest possible guide. I already knew from Pat that it was important to check that the guide was benign by asking, "Are you from the light?" three times, but I hadn't realized that 'lesser' benign guides could show up unless you ask for the best.

This made sense of the fact that I hadn't really got on with a guide that had appeared when I asked for help with writing a year or two before. He told me his name was Moravian, and I imagined him to be a Victorian occultist, dressed in a dark suit and top hat. Although he was well meaning, there was something a bit severe and pushy about him. He certainly did not encourage me or bring out the best in me (rather, I felt chided for not doing well enough) and so I didn't pursue the connection.

But this time it was entirely different. Following the steps in the book, I called upon my highest guide from the light and my new guide made her presence known (I could tell that she was a she). Her approach was gentle, yet as I opened to her presence, her energy was so powerful that I was almost swooning in her cloud-like atmosphere of pure love-bliss. I could happily let go, fall down – die! I could surrender, sigh away a lifetime of tension, breathe out and never need to breathe in again. Oh this was SUBLIME!

Although I couldn't exactly *see* her, I knew she was made entirely of white light, was about 10 feet tall, had long hair and was wearing flowing robes. And yes, she had wings – she was an angel! Fortunately, I had long ceased caring that my imagination usually comes up with archetypal clichés, and simply allowed myself to fall in soul-love with the most divinely, beautiful creature I had ever encountered.

She told me her name was Clarion (which I thought was odd, but really liked) and she has been with me ever since.

Finding Guidance in a Crisis

It is one of those awful times of intense distress and you don't know what to do with yourself. There's no one you can talk to right now and you are on your own.

Perhaps you are in heartache having just split up with your partner. Or learned that you are being made redundant from a job you love. Or you have finally hit a financial wall and heard that you may lose your house. Maybe you've had a scene with your wayward teenager. Or you've had some bad news about a health issue. Or been let down by a friend. You are feeling traumatized, angry, grief-stricken, frightened, anxious, and hopeless. And most of all, you feel alone.

Where do you turn? What on earth can you do? Well, there is something...

The process below evolved from my own experience of dealing with acute feelings of emotional upset. I am a natural communicator; I like to talk through issues and problems until they are resolved. But sometimes talking won't do it, or isn't available.

One night, Pat and I had a heated disagreement that wasn't resolved by bedtime. He went to bed, but I couldn't bear to be near him when we felt so estranged and I certainly couldn't sleep. Knowing I couldn't talk to my beloved best friend and confidant (as he was at most other times) was as though the sun had been extinguished and I had been plunged into the most desolate and dark winter. I stayed up, feeling alone, tormented and at my wits' end.

I was desperate to talk to somebody, but it was late at night. Then I thought of taking out my journal and writing it all down. And so I ranted, raved, wept, scrawled and scribbled furiously – all the frustration, all the confusion, all the self-doubt. I asked impossible to answer questions, wrote appallingly insulting things, swore, scratched huge exclamation and question marks. It all poured out uninhibitedly, the good, the bad and the ugly, splattering the mess out, right there on the page. SO THERE!

Eventually, I stopped. There was nothing left to say. I had vented everything out of me and was fully expressed, empty. Having finally given myself permission to accept exactly the way I felt, judgmental warts and all, the raging storm suddenly abated. A strange peacefulness fell upon me, and in that whisper pause of a moment, I became aware of a loving presence in the room with me.

I couldn't see anything, and wasn't sure where this presence was, but could sense an atmosphere, a density, and had a tangible feeling that 'someone' was there with me. Needing a workable concept to describe what was happening, my mind helpfully framed this to be a guardian angel, spirit guide or higher self (it didn't seem to matter which). Whatever it was, it felt lovely and I totally trusted it.

The most incredible thing about the experience was the way this guiding presence *felt*. There was a tangible atmosphere seeping into me as though I was being tenderly wrapped in a blanket of pure love. My body relaxed, my mind cleared and my heart opened. All three – body, mind and heart – were sighing in sweet surrender.

It seemed completely natural to communicate with this presence, and so, with the innocence of a child, I tentatively began to 'talk' to 'it' via writing. My side of the dialogue came through in normal lower case letters and the reply side from the presence in capital letters, somehow denoting a different voice and personality. I was amazed at what came back to me.

Hardly mattering what the answers were, the experience of communing with this pure love was all the answer I needed anyway. However, answers did come – remarkable, surprising, wise answers from a completely loving perspective. My guide explained where Pat was coming from in a way that made my anger and frustration with him melt. I could only see him with the eyes of love now too, and all I felt was tenderness, under-standing and compassion.

I understood myself completely, I understood him completely and I understood the conflict we were having completely too. All the tension in me left. My heart grew as big as the universe and all was well.

Suddenly, I was overcome with weariness; the same kind of weariness you get when you finally arrive at your destination after a long, arduous journey. All I wanted to do was go to sleep. I could hardly keep my eyes open. So I thanked my guiding presence and said goodbye. I crept into bed, and after gazing upon my sleeping husband with gentle, knowing affection, was asleep in an instant.

The next day, the tension between us had completely evapo-rated. Pat sensed the change in me and there was space for us to feel open to each other again. We were still emotionally bruised and had our disagreement to sort out, but that was so easily done. I simply read out the wise words of my guiding presence which made sense of everything. This gave us both a deeper understanding of what was going on, why we were each triggered in the way we were, and what we each needed to heal and move on.

Step-by-step Guide

And so, my tip for you in a time of crisis, especially when you are alone and have no one to turn to, is this:

1   Vent out all your feelings in writing, uninhibitedly. Be as disgraceful and unreasonable and confused as you like! Write until you are empty and there's nothing more to say.

2   Pause and take a few quiet breaths. Invite a loving presence, a wise guide, your higher self, God, or however

you like to think of it, to show up and support you in this time of need.

3   Check that this presence is good by asking three times, "Are you from the light?" The guiding presence cannot answer "Yes" three times unless it is benevolent. If it cannot answer "Yes" clearly three times, tell it to leave immediately and that it is not wanted. Then repeat steps 2 and 3 again until you get a "Yes" three times.

4   You may ask your guide for their name if you like. (You can also ask your guide for any other information on them, but maybe at another time when you don't have such a pressing issue to resolve.)

5   Talk to this guide and presence in writing (even if you don't believe it is there, or can't explain what it is). Use lower case letters when you are speaking and capital letters when the guiding presence is speaking.

6   When you are finished, thank and acknowledge your guide for their help. Remember you can call upon your guide any time you like.

7   At a later time, revisit what you have written when dialoguing with your guide and apply any good advice or guidance.

Chapter 28

Casting Pearls

Early Thrivecraft

Soon, Pat and I were coaching people one-to-one and running groups and courses. What we found was that there were certain themes that came up for people over and over again. One, of course, is love and relationships. So many people are looking for the right relationship or to improve the one they've got, or to find out if they need to let go of the relationship they are in. Having just experienced our own happy love story, relationship coaching became one branch of Thrivecraft's work and we developed a popular workshop called Get Ready for Love.

I also ran a meditation class, now free from any Buddhist identity. As well as teaching traditional methods, the meditation that I was guiding began to take on different forms. I started to channel new meditations rather than practicing and teaching existing ones. Over a couple of years, I evolved a powerful guided meditation which I eventually named Ask Your Inner Wisdom. This meditation allows you to drop into your own source of inner wisdom and find wise answers and intuitive solutions to questions and problems.

By the autumn of 2003, Thrivecraft was establishing well and Pat and I turned our attention to our wedding. We had a magical Shamanic ceremony on the banks of the river Dart a short stroll from the Sea Trout Inn where we met. Being the location of "I see you" and our first kiss, we had our reception there. A Scottish bagpiper led the wedding procession up the hill from the river to the inn. Then, about two hundred of us dined and danced away the evening in the marquee and gardens, blessed by fine 'Indian Summer' weather.

Alchemy

The next 10 years of Thrivecraft and married life brought Pat and me many rich and vivid experiences. As well as the enormous reward of our vocation and the many wonderful people we were working with and befriending, there were challenges. During 2005, Pat's health broke down and he was forced to stop working. There followed an intense few years adapting to the changes and caring for Pat until his health stabilized (though not enough for him to return to work, and still requiring a degree of care) while I carried on with Thrivecraft on my own.

I was also now a mum to a lively teenage boy who, being dyslexic, didn't find learning easy although he thrived at school socially. Jamie was spending the middle of the week with his dad, and Friday to Monday with us, made simpler when Colin found a home in the same village. Although Pat and I managed to stay in the village, we had to move home three times during these years – including downsizing from a seven room Tudor cottage with a garden house to a pair of caravans in a field – all of which I organized single-handedly. It was a time of emotional, physical and financial demands and of digging deep within and in our relationships.

However, it was also a time of inspiration; an initiation by means of the rite of ordeal that yielded many treasures. Lots of grit in lots of oysters equals lots of pearls! My ability to find and utilize inner wisdom became stronger and stronger, even and especially in these times of challenge.

I had major insights about how to love more and more uncon-ditionally in a committed partnership and what a growing young man needs from a mother in order to flourish. Having put Thrivecraft on the back burner for a while, I carried on solo under my own name, simplifying to mostly one-to-one coaching work and writing. I was also reviewing and figuring out who I was now – what was my 'brand', my unique offering, my message?

Who was it I wanted to reach and serve and with what?

In retrospect (in fact, in writing this chapter), I see these challenging years as my initiation and grounding 'in the world'. All the insights I had gained in the seclusion of the Triratna community now needed to find relevance and application in everyday life dealing with everyday issues like money, health, partnership, motherhood and managing a home. I was well and truly out of the meditation cave and into the thick of ordinary society. Over the years I had often read stories of how 'enlightened' masters are not truly masters until they can apply their wisdom in the everyday world. Now it was my turn to do that.

I came to truly recognize my inner wisdom and the massive contribution all those years of meditation and spiritual practice made to those I was working with as well as my own life. It was around now that my colleagues started to refer to me as "the Inner Wisdom Coach" – a tag that went some way to labeling what I was bringing into my vocation and the coaching world. I have to thank my former TV 'Dragon' client, now friend, Rachel Elnaugh, for encouraging me to 'own' my spiritual power and embody inner wisdom as a vital part of my unique brand.

Increasingly, I had the urge to capture and formulate my approach – something accessible and non-Buddhist, yet utilizing all the incredible learning I had from those experiences – and get a body of work out to a much wider audience. Much creativity was pouring through me and I wrote articles and blogs, recorded guided meditations and videos, created new workshops, and exploded into the world of social media with gusto, making many fantastic connections and collaborations, of whom Rachel was one. Increasingly inspired to write books, I scoped out a whole series of book ideas and began to talk to mentors and publishers.

New Pearls

Much of my output came to a halt in 2010, however, when many issues come to a head. During UK's most severe, snowy winter in decades, we spent seven months living in a pair of caravans and dealing with a peak of health, housing, finance and family challenges. Having bravely and successfully met them head on, we finally moved into a secure home in February 2011.

As keen Feng Shui practitioner Rachel informed me, our move coincided with the Chinese New Year of the Rabbit. I was born in the Year of the Rabbit, so it would be a good year for me, Rachel told me. Themes associated with the Rabbit include health, home, money and family, and so it was with great relief that I declared 2011 a year to focus on those very things.

Jamie was now living with us full-time and I was relishing being a full-time mum again and giving him the support he needed, especially during the school week. Pat's health was steady after a new diagnosis and treatment, and I was attending to some health issues of my own with the help of Ayurveda, energy healing, herbal medicine, German New Medicine, EFT and acupuncture.

We had spent some of that snowy winter in Scotland supporting my mum while she went through some intensive medical treatment. By the time of our move, she was completing her treatment and would go on to make a good recovery. With perfect synchronicity, I had an ongoing regular contract with a lovely long-term client that gave me the ideal amount of work while allowing plenty of time for home and family. I was relaxed, happy and finding balance again.

In September 2012, feeling restored and well, I gave my first workshop for more than two years on International Peace Day. I was then inspired to create a local event of my own in tandem with something Rachel was doing in London. On 12-12-12, a date famous for the Mayan prediction that the world would come to an end, Rachel was running a SourceTV event celebrating the spirit of 2012.

In our circles, we chose to look upon 12-12-12 as a time of rebirth into a new paradigm of love and cooperation. In Totnes, Devon, our Unity 2012 Celebration was a sell-out success, bringing many of my friends, clients and colleagues together again. We were all feeling the rising spirit of 2012; a spirit that celebrates the power of the collective to create the kind of world we want to see together. I was beginning to hear a call from my inner wisdom to galvanize Thrivecraft into life again.

My creativity and inspiration were gathering momentum. In February 2013, I celebrated my 49th birthday with friends, inviting them along to my choir practice for the evening and a party afterwards. The combination of singing, friendship, love, affirmation, joy, celebration, and raw chocolate cake resulted in a night of no-sleep-needed divine download for me. I had a scintillating, detailed vision of exactly how and where I wanted to take my work next, and so, the Thrivecraft Academy was conceived.

Over the next two years, I presented a program of monthly Thrivecraft workshops, meditation classes and training courses, packaging up and passing on my entire body of work. It was a huge output, like finally breathing out after breathing in for so long, but I loved it, and danced through the months in a state of joyful, natural creative flow.

To my utter delight, those months saw the creation of more than 50 accredited Thrivecraft Coaches, Practitioners, Meditation Practitioners and Meditation Teachers, plus reached out to many more that dropped in to workshops or classes. In the process Thrivecraft became a registered training provider and was recognized as a modality in its own right. Pat and I had always nurtured this vision of developing a training academy and creating a community of Thrivecraft professionals from the very beginning. Now, 10 or so years later, our Thrivecraft baby had grown up and come of age.

Chapter 29

Trusting the Tides of Inspiration

Riding the Rhythm

Do you trust your own rhythms? Do you allow yourself to do nothing and stare into space just because you feel like it? If a rush of creative ideas wakes you up at night, do you get up and start scribbling or smother it down because 'you must get your sleep'? When all your energy has vanished, do you force yourself to get on with some work or allow yourself to rest?

Observing the ebb and flow of my creative energy after our final big house move in 2011 prompted me to think about this. When we first moved, it was easy to see why I wasn't dreaming up any new workshops or enthusiastically promoting my latest inner wisdom product – I was exhausted! Then the weeks went on and I settled deeply into my inner world, wanting to do little more than meditate and write.

After a while, I started to get a bit concerned. What if all that creative juice has gone? Should I try and drum something up? But no matter how I looked at it, I just did not feel like it. I know from hard experience that it's counterproductive to exhaust myself trying to swim against the tide, but it's not always easy to keep the faith. Nonetheless, this time I managed to wait and trust that the change would come naturally.

Then, eventually, it happened; a huge up-rush of creativity and inspiration came bursting through. Ideas, excitement, enthusiasm and energy came forth aplenty – fully formed and in such abundance – and my new workshops were conceived. A couple of phone calls were made and the people and places I wanted all fell into place beautifully. There was a quality of effortless cooperation with a power so much greater and wiser than myself. My job was to be switched on enough to notice the turning tide, fit enough to get on the surfboard and keep my balance, and from there-on-in simply have a wonderful ride!

To me, one of the greatest gifts of my self-determining lifestyle is the wonderful opportunity to follow my natural rhythms more truly. Sometimes it is an emotional rhythm – feeling slow and sad or fast and excited; sometimes it is intellectual – clear as a bell or dull as dishwater. Then there are physical rhythms prompted by hormonal changes or food, exercise and sleep patterns. And of course there's the environment – the light, the dark, the sun, the moon, the seasons, the weather, the surroundings.

Our bodies and psyches are fantastically engineered sensing machines. Should you pay attention – simply pay attention – you get all the bio/psychic feedback you need in a nanosecond and you will KNOW what is right for you at every turn.

However, if you override this awareness by getting too busy and out of touch with yourself (or giving too much of your power and freedom away to an over-demanding person or job) you lose one of your most precious abilities – to regulate a happy, balanced lifestyle for yourself. What's more, regulating yourself like this is your primary responsibility in life. No one else can do this for you or be blamed if you do not do it for yourself.

However, there is another whole dimension of rhythm in our lives, the ebb and flow of inspiration – our spiritual rhythm. When you are inspired you feel a creative energy rising up within you, giving you the ideas, direction and impetus to make something new happen. It seems to bubble up from inside you even if it is triggered by an external source like an inspiring talk or a sublime piece of music. Sometimes it just seems to come from nowhere.

Only when you have a sense of being in possession of your whole self can inspiration start to come through into an adequate container. Having pulled yourself into some sort of shape, your natural creative energy has a place to be and a vehicle through which to express. It feels like you have a wellspring within you, constantly bubbling up from your deep inner source.

Hence, why, as a coach, I prefer to work with inspiration rather than motivation. As well as being a carrot rather than stick approach, it is a much more empowering and graceful way to work. Helping people ignite their own natural joyful impetus is more independently sustainable than trying to push them up a mountain they would rather not climb.

Sometimes I think we've got it all wrong, that we think we have to 'make' ourselves do stuff because it is 'good for us'. No, no! Spend the time to develop the self-love and find the thing you really want to be doing because you were meant to be doing it. Then it is just a matter of lighting the touchpaper and standing back while an inspired new lifestyle takes off.

Inspiration is a massive force for the good. When you are inspired you are in touch with who you really are and what truly moves you, with love and joy rather than fear and dread. As I was saying earlier, one of my favorite tips is how to tell if you are making the right decision by asking yourself, "Am I making this choice from love or fear?"

Follow Your Bliss

If we only could remember that these three little words, famously coined by Joseph Campbell, hold the key to a truly happy, fulfilled life.

Follow your bliss.

To *follow* means finding the trail and taking one step. Maybe you can't see exactly what your complete destination is, but you get a bit of the picture, a feeling, a general sense of direction. It is okay to take one step and trust that the next step will be revealed. All you need do is ensure that you are still on the path of bliss, that each step feels good – even if you don't know where it is ultimately leading.

It is *your* bliss we are talking about. Not anyone else's. And not what other people think should be yours. What sets *you* alight, turns *you* on, and fills *you* with happiness? You don't have to understand why or justify it to anyone else. You came into the world with your own unique talents, interests and potential. Just stick to what you really love and eventually it will all make sense.

And what is *bliss*? It is something deeper than just immediate gratification. It is an expansive feeling of rightness, truth, freedom, unfolding and fulfillment. Sometimes we do something that we think we want to, but it does not really satisfy us. It feels hollow, like it hasn't really hit the spot. Bliss is a gentle fullness that bubbles up from deep inside and it can't help but spill over and create happiness wherever you go.

And so, if you have a decision to make, take a few breaths and check in with yourself. Am I following my bliss? The decisions we make ultimately come from either love or fear. We create happy, fulfilling lives by making sure we are in a state of love before we make decisions. Then we can be sure that we are following our bliss.

So do keep the faith. You do know what is best for you. Your only responsibility is to cultivate sensitivity to your rhythms and allow inspiration to flow. Of course many of us have busy lives with many demands, but even within that, it is possible to invest a little time developing awareness. Meditation is a brilliant way to do this. Just 10 minutes a day, sitting quietly, feeling your breath move through your body is a wonderful start.

Chapter 30

Pearl Fire

A Return Visit

Loch Voil in the Scottish Highlands was dark and glassy-smooth, reflecting a dynamic 3D sky full of pretty, plump grey and white clouds. Long and deep, the loch (loch being the Scottish name for lake) stretched for miles in both directions; the awe-inspiring wraparound panorama completed by green forests and soft low mountains. It was August 2013 and I was standing on the exact spot by the Dhanakosa Buddhist retreat center in Scotland where I had waved sparklers in the air 20 years before, tracing my new ordained name into the winter night. However, this time, I was standing on the loch side, ready to let the name Srimati go.

I declared out loud my intention to "lovingly lay aside my Buddhist name, Srimati," and threw a large pebble into the water with a definitive splash. Then I made my way to the retreat center itself where I discovered, by sheer chance, that the shrine room was available as they were between retreats for a few hours. I took the opportunity to go inside and conduct my own private ritual in the very same sacred space where I had been publicly ordained and had my ordained name, Srimati, announced in 1993.

Speaking out loud although I was alone, I thanked Triratna, Sangharakshita, my preceptor Sanghadevi and all my spiritual friends, and formally put my Buddhist name down. With a final bow to the Buddha statue on the shrine, Srimati, 'Radiant Mind', ceremonially became Maggie Kay, 'Pearl Fire', again.

On our way up through Scotland a week before, Pat and I spent a night in Mauchline in Ayrshire, in the home town of my maternal great-great gran, Mary Kay. Feeling deeply connected with my mum's lineage and the name Kay that we shared and I was about to take back, I shed a tear as I toasted my ancestors at our evening meal.

In the morning, we visited the house where Mary Kay lived and gave birth to her daughter (also named Mary Kay) and to the 'big house' where she worked as a dairy maid. Being a single mother, she eventually allowed her toddler to be adopted by my great-granny Reid who was an informal midwife and healer in the district and had no children of her own.

Pat and I then went on to Mauchline cemetery and spent a peaceful and meaningful hour there. Pat left me alone to wander and muse and I meditated for a while. The spirit of the younger Mary Kay, my gran's mum, came powerfully into my awareness as though she was speaking to me.

She told me that my name change was purposeful and welcome, that I had some ancestral business to complete and that becoming Maggie Kay again would help me do this. It would also help get my teachings about inner wisdom out to those who would benefit from them, something that was part of my soul purpose should I choose to fulfill it.

Continuing on our trip, Pat and I spent a lovely few days with my mum on the small island where she now lives with my stepdad Jim. When Mum took me in her arms to greet me she murmured, "Aw, welcome home, Maggie Kay," with special affection. She was delighted that I was reclaiming the names she had lovingly given me at birth. I surrendered into her warm embrace like a child. It is not that I was ever aware of being estranged from my family, but in that moment, I felt like a returning prodigal daughter.

We spent the last night of our special holiday at a hotel near the retreat center, the very same hotel where Pat shared with me his "walking away from themselves" meditation experience in 2002. It seemed significant that we had stayed there after Gran's ash scattering ceremony, and here we were again to change my

name back to Maggie Kay. The following morning we called in at
the retreat center on the loch where the retrieval of my original
family names became complete.

Letting Go of Srimati

It was unusual for resigning Order Members to keep their
Buddhist name (actually, it was unusual for Order Members to
resign at all), but when I resigned from the Order in 2002, I felt I
was still Srimati and couldn't imagine going back to my old
name. Everyone knew me as Srimati, it was even on official
documents, and the name was very precious to me.

So I asked my preceptor, Sanghadevi, if I had her blessing to
keep using Srimati and she said yes. As far as she was concerned,
as long as I was still aspiring towards spiritual enlightenment in
some way, she was happy to give her blessing. I thought her
attitude reflected the true spirit of Buddhism – practical, non-
dogmatic, and tolerant – and I was glad to leave the Order with
good grace and a beautiful name.

By 2010, however, I started considering dropping Srimati and
reverting to Maggie Kay, a version of my original name that both
honored the past and was fresh for today. One way or another, I
kept tripping over the 'Buddhist-ness' of Srimati and was increasingly wondering if having an unusual, hard to remember, Indian
language spiritual name put a barrier between me and the people
I wanted to reach with Thrivecraft. Plus I wasn't a Buddhist
anymore, so why have a Buddhist name?

One or two close friends had strong feelings that a change to
Maggie Kay was right, notably my dear friend and coach buddy,
Terry Brightwater, whose deeply insightful support proved to be
invaluable during the process of change that followed. My mum
had never been keen about my being called Srimati instead of the
names she had christened me, and believed Maggie Kay would
be better for my professional work.

However, changing my name because it would be good for business wasn't enough of a reason for me. It needed to be more personal and meaningful than that. In the end, a challenging communication with a colleague catalyzed the change. As I contemplated why I was so stirred up about the issue (with the help of a session with my dear friend and healer Bill Tucker), I came upon the realization that I was still unconsciously but powerfully 'renouncing' the material world, something that was inherent in my ordination vows.

Speaking with Pat about my insights, he suddenly voiced what had also come upon me that very morning, "I think it might be time to stop being Srimati." As soon as he said it, I knew he was absolutely right. It was time. By putting down the name Srimati I was finally breaking the Buddhist vow of renunciation. And by picking up my old name, I was welcoming myself back into the world again – spiritually and materially – and reopening the power and magic of my natural human and family inheritance.

Always Me, Not Me

As a baby, lying in my cot in my attic bedroom, I can remember how the room looked through the bars of my cot – the sloping ceiling, the skylight window, the cream painted woodchip wallpaper. But what is strange about the memory is that, despite being a tiny baby, unable to walk or talk, I felt then EXACTLY as I feel now.

It was the same essential 'me' looking out of the cot, the same big, wise, loving me that I always was and I always will be, a timeless, limitless, deeply contented free consciousness, not fettered by anything. And once that memory came back to me, I could recognize that same essence, that knowing, that never ending 'me-ness' throughout every stage of my life. I can feel it right now within me. It is always there.

Paradoxically, one of the most profound insights I ever had (which came on a retreat, not long before I was ordained) showed me that there was no 'me'. I realized that "I did not *own* my life." Those were the words that came to me.

What this means is that I can step outside of my life story and my identity with it and see myself as though I am someone else, without any particular investment in it. Certain features and circumstances come together – personality, history, habits, talents, physical body, challenges, relationships, anxieties, conditioning – and result in how I experience life in any given moment. That's all 'I' am: a temporary participant in a unique moment of ever-changing conditions. There is no 'I'!

This perspective is quite hard to describe, but the result of it in my life, when I am in touch with it, is that I feel free to be absolutely brilliant or totally terrible (or somewhere in between) and it doesn't matter!

If I do amazing things, I can enjoy and appreciate them because it is 'not me' and being big-headed or modest is irrelevant. If I fail or do badly at something, likewise, I can feel compassion for the poor soul who messed up as it is 'not me'. Well it is me, but only because 'I' am embodying that particular combination of circumstances and energies in that moment. Anybody else would be the same in the same conditions. So it is not something I need to pin my sense of who I am or my self-esteem on.

So through my various names and identities – Margaret for my first 11 years, Kay throughout my teens and 20s, Srimati for the next two decades and then Maggie Kay since 2013 – I have been experiencing this paradoxical sense of being essentially the same 'me' and fundamentally 'not me', all at the same time.

Fortunately, Buddhist wisdom is full of these paradoxes, for example, Ashvaghosha's well-known observation that: "Nothing really exists, nor does it not exist, nor at once does it exist and not exist, nor at once doesn't it exist and not exist." And so I am at home with this consciousness expanding style of contemplation and have arrived at making sense of the question, 'who am I?'

Dive for Your Pearls

When we connect with and recognize our true, never ending, ever changing, formless self, we open a channel to our inner wisdom. More than this, we connect with THE true, eternal formless wisdom of the universe – whether we meet it as inner or outer wisdom. To do this, we need only drop down for a moment into silence, dive into the deep ocean of peace, and there our oysters and pearls will be waiting.

Once we have made this dive a few times we can relate to our everyday personality, our habitual self, with a bit more loving detachment, wearing it like a set of favorite clothes rather than mistaking the clothes for who we really are. We learn to trust the silence of the deep and the wisdom that speaks from there, hearing its voice when we are back on the surface more and more clearly.

Directed by that wisdom and adorned with its pearls, we can enjoy our adventures on land, and our unique personality finds more and more joy and healthy expression, however we choose to do that. And this, of course, equips us to find and attract the best and most fulfilling relationships.

I hope you have enjoyed my story and tips and are feeling inspired, encouraged and supported – wherever you are in your own exploration of love and wisdom. This book is packed with teachings, so feel free to reread it again and again. And if you haven't done so already, do revisit some of the practical guide chapters, and try out the recommendations that appeal to you.

If there is one new thing you take away from reading this book, however, I hope it is this – take a few minutes every day to tune in to your inner wisdom. Use my 'Ask Your Inner Wisdom' guided meditation, or just simply 'pause, breathe and ask' on a daily basis.

As you may discover, such a simple but powerful wisdom practice can yield many treasures – clarity, peace, fulfillment, creativity and confidence, to name a few – not least the ability to find and attract your own true love and deep dive together in this wondrous ocean of life.

I wish you all the best with your adventures. Happy diving!

Appendix

Ask Your Inner Wisdom Meditation

To help you access your own inner wisdom very simply and easily, I have created a special meditation, Ask Your Inner Wisdom. It combines many elements of different kinds of meditation and inspiration that I have practiced for over 30 years.

Ask Your Inner Wisdom channeled through me spontaneously, coming from a source much bigger than just my everyday self. It seems entirely appropriate that this beautiful, powerful meditation should perhaps have originated from my own inner wisdom.

As the fastest and most direct way I have come across to connect with inner wisdom, Ask Your Inner Wisdom is very special. It expresses and accesses the core message of all that I teach and share.

To download your free MP3 audio of the 20-minute version of Ask Your Inner Wisdom, go to my website at maggiekaywisdom.com and sign up.

References

Books and Audios (in order of mention)

Bikshu Sangharakshita
Peace is a Fire: A Collection of Writings and Sayings
Windhorse Publications; New Edition (1 April 1995)

Richard Rudd
Gene Keys: Unlocking the Higher Purpose Hidden in Your DNA
Watkins Publishing LTD (9 May 2013)

Esther and Jerry Hicks
Ask and It Is Given: Learning to Manifest the Law of Attraction –
Learning to Manifest Your Desires
Hay House; Second Printing edition (8 January 2010)

Dr. Wayne W. Dyer
Meditations for Manifesting: Morning and Evening Meditations
to Literally Create Your Heart's Desire – Audio CD
Hay House UK; Unabridged edition (1 July 2004)

Clarissa Pinkola Estés
Women Who Run with the Wolves: Contacting the Power of the
Wild Woman
Rider; Classic Ed edition (7 February 2008)

Eckhart Tolle
The Power of Now: A Guide to Spiritual Enlightenment
Yellow Kite (1 February 2001)

Stephen and Ondrea Levine
Embracing the Beloved: Relationship as a Path of Awakening
Gateway (1 April 1995)

Oriah Mountain Dreamer
The Invitation
HarperONE, San Francisco (8 December 1999)

Foundation for Inner Peace
A Course in Miracles
Foundation for Inner Peace; 3rd edition (21 May 2008)

Neale Donald Walsch
Conversations with God, Book 1: An Uncommon Dialogue
Hodder and Stoughton; New Ed edition (6 February 1997)

Arnold M. Patent
You Can Have It All, 4th Rev. Ed.: A Simple Guide to a Joyful and Abundant Life
Celebration Publishing; Revised edition (1 April 2007)

Sanaya Roman and Duane Packer
Opening to Channel: How to Connect with Your Guide (Birth into Light)
H J Kramer; 1 edition (1 April 1987)

BOOKS

O-BOOKS

SPIRITUALITY

O is a symbol of the world, of oneness and unity; this eye represents knowledge and insight. We publish titles on general spirituality and living a spiritual life. We aim to inform and help you on your own journey in this life. If you have enjoyed this book, why not tell other readers by posting a review on your preferred book site? Recent bestsellers from O-Books are:

Heart of Tantric Sex
Diana Richardson
Revealing Eastern secrets of deep love and intimacy to Western couples.
Paperback: 978-1-90381-637-0 ebook: 978-1-84694-637-0

Crystal Prescriptions
The A-Z guide to over 1,200 symptoms and their healing crystals
Judy Hall
The first in the popular series of five books, this handy little guide is packed as tight as a pill-bottle with crystal remedies for ailments.
Paperback: 978-1-90504-740-6 ebook: 978-1-84694-629-5

Take Me To Truth
Undoing the Ego
Nouk Sanchez, Tomas Vieira
The best-selling step-by-step book on shedding the Ego, using
the teachings of *A Course In Miracles*.
Paperback: 978-1-84694-050-7 ebook: 978-1-84694-654-7

The 7 Myths about Love...Actually!
The journey from your HEAD to the HEART of your SOUL
Mike George
Smashes all the myths about LOVE.
Paperback: 978-1-84694-288-4 ebook: 978-1-84694-682-0

The Holy Spirit's Interpretation of the New Testament
A course in Understanding and Acceptance
Regina Dawn Akers
Following on from the strength of *A Course In Miracles*, NTI
teaches us how to experience the love and oneness of God.
Paperback: 978-1-84694-085-9 ebook: 978-1-78099-083-5

The Message of A Course In Miracles
A translation of the text in plain language
Elizabeth A. Cronkhite
A translation of *A Course In Miracles* into plain, everyday
language for anyone seeking inner peace. The companion
volume, *Practicing A Course In Miracles*, offers practical lessons
and mentoring.
Paperback: 978-1-84694-319-5 ebook: 978-1-84694-642-4

Rising in Love
My Wild and Crazy Ride to Here and Now, with Amma, the
Hugging Saint
Ram Das Batchelder
Rising in Love conveys an author's extraordinary journey of

spiritual awakening with the Guru, Amma.
Paperback: 978-1-78279-687-9 ebook: 978-1-78279-686-2

Thinker's Guide to God
Peter Vardy
An introduction to key issues in the philosophy of religion.
Paperback: 978-1-90381-622-6

Your Simple Path
Find happiness in every step
Ian Tucker
A guide to helping us reconnect with what is really important in
our lives.
Paperback: 978-1-78279-349-6 ebook: 978-1-78279-348-9

365 Days of Wisdom
Daily Messages To Inspire You Through The Year
Dadi Janki
Daily messages which cool the mind, warm the heart and guide
you along your journey.
Paperback: 978-1-84694-863-3 ebook: 978-1-84694-864-0

Body of Wisdom
Women's Spiritual Power and How it Serves
Hilary Hart
Bringing together the dreams and experiences of women across
the world with today's most visionary spiritual teachers.
Paperback: 978-1-78099-696-7 ebook: 978-1-78099-695-0

Dying to Be Free
From Enforced Secrecy to Near Death to True Transformation
Hannah Robinson
After an unexpected accident and near-death experience,
Hannah Robinson found herself radically transforming her life,

while a remarkable new insight altered her relationship with her father; a practising Catholic priest.
Paperback: 978-1-78535-254-6 ebook: 978-1-78535-255-3

The Ecology of the Soul
A Manual of Peace, Power and Personal Growth for Real People in the Real World
Aidan Walker
Balance your own inner Ecology of the Soul to regain your natural state of peace, power and wellbeing.
Paperback: 978-1-78279-850-7 ebook: 978-1-78279-849-1

Not I, Not other than I
The Life and Teachings of Russel Williams
Steve Taylor, Russel Williams
The miraculous life and inspiring teachings of one of the World's greatest living Sages.
Paperback: 978-1-78279-729-6 ebook: 978-1-78279-728-9

On the Other Side of Love
A Woman's Unconventional Journey Towards Wisdom
Muriel Maufroy
When life has lost all meaning, what do you do?
Paperback: 978-1-78535-281-2 ebook: 978-1-78535-282-9

Practicing A Course In Miracles
A Translation of the Workbook in Plain Language and With Mentoring Notes
Elizabeth A. Cronkhite
The practical second and third volumes of The Plain-Language *A Course in Miracles*.
Paperback: 978-1-84694-403-1 ebook: 978-1-78099-072-9

Readers of ebooks can buy or view any of these bestsellers by clicking on the live link in the title. Most titles are published in paperback and as an ebook. Paperbacks are available in traditional bookshops. Both print and ebook formats are available online.

Find more titles and sign up to our readers' newsletter at http://www.johnhuntpublishing.com/mind-body-spirit

Follow us on Facebook at https://www.facebook.com/OBooks/ and Twitter at https://twitter.com/obook